LOREN CUN

WIT

Is That Really You,
GOD?

HEARING THE VOICE OF GOD

y**WAM**
P U B L I S H I N G
P.O. BOX 55787   SEATTLE, WA 98155

Ian Thompson
Jan. 08
YWAM Arctic
Mercy

YWAM Publishing is the publishing ministry of Youth With A Mission. Youth With A Mission (YWAM) is an international missionary organization of Christians from many denominations dedicated to presenting Jesus Christ to this generation. To this end, YWAM has focused its efforts in three main areas: (1) training and equipping believers for their part in fulfilling the Great Commission (Matthew 28:19), (2) personal evangelism, and (3) mercy ministry (medical and relief work).

For a free catalog of books and materials, contact:

YWAM Publishing
P.O. Box 55787, Seattle, WA 98155
(425) 771-1153 or (800) 922-2143
www.ywampublishing.com

Is That Really You, God?
Copyright ©1984, 2001 by Loren Cunningham
Second Edition

10 09 08 07 06   10 9 8 7 6 5

Published by YWAM Publishing
P.O. Box 55787, Seattle, WA 98155

ISBN 1-57658-244-2

Printed in the United States of America.

Contents

With deep gratitude…

Janice Rogers and I wish to thank the many friends who have made this book possible. Especially Linda Bond, Lori Bragg, June Coxhead, Katherine Ewing, Jeff Fountain, Sandy Grey, Dodie Gunderson, Becky King, Diane Koppen, Kristen Meidal, Joe Portale, Jim Rogers, Barbara Thompson, and Nancy Wade. We also thank the dozens of people who spent hours being interviewed for background information. Special honor and thanks go to our friend John Sherrill for his labor of love in overseeing this project.

A Word About
the Supernatural

THIS is a book about the outright supernatural.

And I, for one, am ready for it.

When my wife, Elizabeth, and I coauthored some of the early books of the Renewal Movement (*The Cross and the Switchblade, God's Smuggler, The Hiding Place*), we included accounts of mystery and miracle, not because they were sensational but because without them, the events we were reporting could not have happened. For the past decade, the emphasis in American publishing has shifted somewhat toward the believer's need for personal commitment and discipline.

But the pendulum is swinging back again, as it always must, from the truth of our responsibility to the twin truth of God's initiative. This book by Loren Cunningham is full of startling evidence of God's sovereign activity in our lives today. So inexplicable, in fact, in human terms, were Loren's experiences that he and his coauthor, Janice Rogers, and I made a decision. We went through the manuscript, eliminating instances of miraculous guidance that could not be verified by "two or three witnesses" (the Bible's own standard for accuracy).

I include myself in this decision because I acted as editorial consultant on the project, living for weeks at a time on one of the 113 worldwide Youth With A Mission (YWAM) bases, overseeing the writing of the book. It was a new experiment in teaching-by-doing, and out of it I believe has come a fine new author, Loren's sister Janice Rogers. Janice has done a sensitive job in blending a good narrative with solid teaching on a subject of central importance to every Christian: "How can I learn to recognize the voice of God?"

One problem the three of us never did solve—just what and who to include out of so many superb stories (many of them old YWAM favorites), so many people who seemed essential to the narrative, and so many teachers who just could not be left out! I finally stepped in as the outsider and made the bound-to-be-unpopular choice. Since we can't tell the whole story—not in a dozen books this length—this sampling will have to represent riches only hinted at here.

So if you already know YWAM, don't look for your own favorite memory—it probably won't be here. And if you *don't* already know YWAM, you have an adventure in store! A first look at a God who moves in power in human lives. A God who waits to be invited into yours....

JOHN SHERRILL

Chosen Books
Lincoln, Virginia

ONE

All That Glitters...

I BOUNDED up the wide marble steps of Aunt Sandra's Palm Beach home, settled on the shore of Lake Worth, which she and Uncle George had purchased from a member of the Vanderbilt family. The Florida night was illuminated by floodlights set among tropical foliage and by the golden hue cast from the tall windows of the house.

A moment after I rang the bell at the double doors, Hawkins, cold and formal as usual, threw the bolt and ushered me into the marble foyer graced with statues and Grecian urns.

"Good evening, Master Loren." Hawkins still called me *Master Loren*, even though I was twenty-six years old! "Mrs. Meehan will join you in the library."

"Thank you, Hawkins. You are looking well."

Hawkins bowed slightly, led me into the library, and went to find my aunt. Of all the twenty rooms in Aunt Sandra's winter home, I liked the library best, with its Persian rug and its floor-to-ceiling bookcases, its muted greens and browns.

"You'll never belong here, though," I whispered to myself, catching a glimpse of my image in a mirror behind one of the wing-backed chairs.

The light hit me at an angle, and I could still see the shadow of acne scars left over from my teenage years, so recently behind me. If I had come to live with Aunt Sandra, as she had wanted, I'd have gone to an expensive dermatologist. My hair, wavy and dark brown, did not have that bleached-out look of the usual Palm Beach sun fans. I was fashionably lanky, as was Aunt Sandra, but not for the right reasons, I'm afraid. I just had not eaten much on this trip around the world.

My eyes fell on a huge illuminated world globe that stood by Uncle George's favorite dark leather chair. For the briefest moment, I saw again the strange vision that had been haunting my life for six years now, ever since I was twenty. The vision was of wave upon wave of young people like me, missionaries still in their teens and early twenties, marching onto the shores of all the continents of the world.... The vision was tantalizing. What brashness made me think it was a mandate from the Lord? A lot of people get "visions." Could mine really be one of those special guiding events that launch a great work for God? If I tried to suggest that to sensible Aunt Sandra, I knew it would threaten her.

Aunt Sandra walked in, followed by her dog, Gail. "Welcome back, dear!" Aunt Sandra glided across the Persian rug, her quiet grace and elegance a contrast to the boxer who bounded up to me. Aunt Sandra and my father had been raised in the same poor itinerant preacher's home. Of all the adjectives you could use about their childhoods, elegant was not a candidate.

"It's really good to have you here. George will be home later," she said.

Uncle George, I knew, would still be at his club. George Meehan had made his fortune in textiles before settling down to a rhythm of summers in Lake Placid, winters in Palm Beach, and autumns and springs in Providence, Rhode Island. My most vivid memory of Uncle George was of seeing him practice golf at the summer mansion by driving a bucketful of balls into the lake. That was Uncle George.

"Loren," Aunt Sandra was saying, "I know you must be exhausted. But first, how about a bedtime snack?"

It was a standing joke, my love for the delicacies of their cook. A maid brought the food in, and while I ate hungrily and Aunt Sandra nibbled, I told her about my exploratory trip around the world. I'd been trying to understand the meaning of that strange vision of young missionaries.

Aunt Sandra was not too interested in what I had to say. She had been so turned off by Christianity during her childhood, and now she wanted to leave it behind. She listened absently to my story, but when I paused, she quickly cut in.

"I'm glad for you, Loren," she said, standing. "It's good for young people to get these things out of their systems. We have a lot to talk about, but you've come a long way today. We can take it up in the morning."

Making my way upstairs to the large bedroom that had become mine, I knew very well what Aunt Sandra wanted to talk about: a generous offer from Uncle George. Strangely I didn't look forward to it. I slipped between the carefully turned-back silk sheets and lay there worrying while the moon's blue shadows moved around the room. Tomorrow I'd have to tell my aunt that the Lord had spoken to me.

I folded my arms behind my head and stared at the dark ceiling. How do you explain that you have heard the voice of God to someone who has been hurt already by such strange-sounding pronouncements? Before I tried to tell my aunt, I had better be sure I was looking honestly, really honestly, at guidance—including the parts that had turned off Aunt Sandra.

Hearing God's voice had more than once brought my family and me to turning points that changed lives. My dad's father owned a successful laundry in Uvalde, Texas, and was living comfortably when he received what he termed a "call" to preach. He put his business up for sale. "You're a fool, I'll say it outright," said Granddad's brother, to which Granddad replied, "If I heard God right and didn't obey, that's when I'd be the fool."

I have always been intrigued by what happened next. At first Granddad obeyed his call in a part-time fashion, taking a string of jobs in various towns in Texas and preaching on weekends. Then tragedy hit. He and his family were living in San Antonio in 1916 when a dreaded smallpox epidemic broke out. His wife and two sons (there were two young boys and three older girls in the family) were stricken with the ter-rifying pox. Granddad went to the hospital isolation ward to live with his sick wife and little boys.

For two weeks Granddad Cunningham maintained his vigil by the beds of his wife and sons. At last the disease seemed to be abating. Granddad got word to the three girls to get everything tidy, because soon they'd be coming home.

But then with terrifying swiftness, his wife's condition changed for the worse. Everyone stood by helplessly as she struggled, and weakened, and then drew her last breath. The authorities insisted on burying Grandmother immediately, right from the hospital. A few hours later, stunned and weep-ing, Granddad and the two boys rode home in the same ambulance that was supposed to have brought Grandmother back. The three girls came running out happily.

"Where's Mother?" they asked. When Granddad told them she had died, the oldest girl, Arnette, screamed and ran into the house. The younger girls, Gertrude and Sandra, held each other and cried. But the trauma was not over. That same day, health authorities arrived at Granddad's house and announced that the mattresses and clothing had to be dragged into the yard and burned. In one day Granddad and his family lost everything but one another. And in a sense they even lost one another because of what happened next.

Incredibly, Granddad Cunningham announced, not long after the cumulative tragedy, that he was going to start preaching full time. And here is the part of Granddad's story that gave Aunt Sandra so much trouble. Hearing God is not all that difficult. If we know the Lord, we have already heard His voice—after all, it was the inner leading that brought us to Him in the first place. But we can hear His voice once and still miss His best if we don't keep on listening. After the *what* of guidance come the *when* and the *how*. Granddad obeyed the what of his call—to preach the Gospel—but failed to seek further guidance as to how God wanted him to do that. If he had, perhaps the ensuing conflicts that his family struggled with would have been far less painful.

Granddad saw himself as a traveling teacher. He couldn't take five children on the road with him, so he placed them in different homes—first with relatives, later with farmer friends who took them in for the chores they could do. In those days, if a child had a roof over his head and three meals a day, people reckoned he was being cared for. Granddad's own five reacted to his decision very individually. Two had more or less neutral responses as the years passed. My aunts Sandra and Arnette blamed their difficult, tearing childhoods on what they saw as Granddad's foolish call. They decided that they would have nothing at all to do with this kind of

Christianity. As soon as they were old enough, they each struck out on their own and went into business, determined to make as much money as they possibly could. To them, that was their solution to the loss of mother and home. They succeeded, too. Aunt Arnette did well, but Aunt Sandra had spectacular success, living eventually in three mansions.

And my own father, Tom, the older of the two boys?

Incredibly, after a hard upbringing in nine different foster homes, Dad never blamed Granddad for obeying the call to preach. In fact, by the time he was seventeen, Dad knew that he, too, had a call. He began to travel with Granddad, holding revival meetings throughout the Southwest.

Dad's decision was followed, as perhaps decisions usually are, by a challenge. Dad received a rare letter from his oldest sister, Arnette, who was living in Miami. He opened the envelope, pulling out a page of Arnette's angular writing. If he would finish high school, Arnette said, she would pay his way through college so that he could earn an engineering degree. He knew it was a great opportunity. But he also knew it would take him away from his calling. Dad thanked Arnette for her generous offer but told her he couldn't accept it.

Arnette's reaction was swift and brutal. "If you are going to tramp through life living off charity, with religion as an excuse," she wrote, "I'm through with you!"

The words stung because they seemed to fit—especially as Dad started helping Granddad with his evangelistic meetings. Granddad never graduated to the more comfortable places. He wanted to help the small, struggling groups of people, and often the only things they could give as payment were canned goods or fresh produce or, occasionally, a chicken. In one place, Granddad and Dad ate stewed apples three times a day without sugar or spice—for two weeks.

After three years of meager fare, Dad was tired of it all. He was nineteen, and although he still considered himself called to preach, he figured he'd wait awhile. He left Granddad and found a good job in Oklahoma City, working on a construction crew high atop the new Biltmore Hotel.

One day, while he was perched on a six-inch-wide girder on the twenty-fourth floor, he watched the giant crane bring up a load of lumber. Suddenly the load swerved straight toward him. He grabbed as the load hit him and in the next instant was dangling in space, desperately holding on while other workmen yelled and hollered. When he got back down, Dad had already made up his mind about one thing: He gave his boss two weeks' notice, then found Granddad and rejoined him for ministry on the road.

Dad never forgot the close brush with death. He had been given a second chance, and this time he was determined to obey God's voice *now*, not at some point in the future when he felt more like it.

TWO

Family Inheritance

WHEN my father, Tom Cunningham, with his square face and dark wavy hair, played his guitar and sang in Granddad's meetings, he had no trouble attracting girls.

There was one exception, however.

One day my father and Granddad found themselves in a small Oklahoma town where another family of traveling evangelists also was holding meetings. The Nicholsons' story was colorful.

The peppery-witted father, Rufus Nicholson, had been an Oklahoma sharecropper when, at age forty, he gave up his occasional bout of hard drinking, responded to the call of Jesus, piled his family into a covered wagon, and began preaching. When Jewell, the third of the Nicholsons' five children, was twelve years old, she was praying on the creek bank late one summer afternoon. Suddenly she heard God speak to her in a clear voice. It didn't surprise Jewell to hear God speaking. People at their camp meetings testified regularly to the experience. Now, God was telling her, "I want you to preach

My Gospel." By the time she was seventeen, Jewell had become one of the regular preachers in the Nicholson clan.

When Tom Cunningham met Jewell Nicholson, he was fascinated by the willowy girl with the snapping black eyes and blunt tongue. He began to court her, but Jewell was so preoccupied with her own call that at first she paid him scant attention. He persisted for months until Jewell finally warmed up to him. Then he posed the important question, and they were married in a simple ceremony in Yellville, Arkansas. Tom had to borrow three dollars for the license.

As newlyweds, my dad and mom began traveling from town to town, preaching on the streets or under temporary shelters made of poles overlaid with tree branches, which people called "brush arbors."

Those were lean days when my parents were first married. Their possessions consisted of an eight-year-old Chevy, a few musical instruments, some clothes, and, of course, their Bibles. With these provisions, they fully expected to do the work of God, and do it efficiently. Which, of course, meant hearing Him with clarity. Both Dad and Mom talked a lot about guidance and the important part it played in having a fruitful ministry. They were familiar with the "inner voice," at times quite audible, at other times more of an impression that came fully formed to the mind. They were familiar, too, with hearing Him speak through Scripture as well as through dreams and visions.

The high purpose of guidance, Dad kept saying, was to tell people about Jesus. "We're fulfilling an urgent command of Jesus Himself," Dad would say when he and Mom talked about the guidance they sought. "The Great Commission, that's the key. 'Go into all the world and preach the Gospel.'" If God did, in fact, commission individuals to the task of going everywhere and telling people the Good News, He would surely guide them.

My parents went wherever they believed God told them to go. They drove to meetings in snowstorms and freezing rains and lived out of the back of automobiles. They lived off whatever the congregation felt like giving them or the coins folks would throw at their feet if they spoke on the street. But leanness was of small consequence, because all the while they were learning to hear the voice of God and obey. With this sense of adventure in following God's direction, they managed to found three churches, all of which are still in existence today.

In the meantime Mom and Dad's family was coming along. My sister Phyllis was born in 1933. Two years later I was born in Taft, California, but my earliest memories are of a dusty Arizona desert town and the sixteen-foot-square tent-house with boxes as furniture. I never felt deprived, however. In fact, I grew up feeling privileged.

My parents were building a church for a group of sixty parishioners. With their own hands they made all the adobe bricks, which they dried in the sun and used for the walls of the church.

They included us in their work and in the process of learning to listen to God. Very early, at the age of six, I had a personal experience in hearing God after a Sunday night meeting, and I knew for the first time that I belonged to Him. But it was hearing His voice in *everyday* happenings— Monday through Sunday—that meant so much to me! One of these events occurred when I was nine and we were living in Covina, California, an orange-tree-filled hamlet thirty-five miles east of Los Angeles.

It was almost dinnertime one evening, and I came running into the house, letting the front screen door slam. My sister Phyllis, eleven years old, quickly reminded me with a finger to her lips that our new baby sister, Janice, was asleep in the next room. I wandered into the kitchen where Mom was taking some cornbread out of the oven. I lifted the lid of a big pot on the stove, sniffing the delicious aroma of red beans and salt pork.

"Loren, we're out of milk. Can you go over to the widow's store and buy some?" Mom didn't have any change—just a single five-dollar bill. "Now be careful with this. That's our grocery money for the week."

I stuck the bill into the pocket of my jeans, whistled for Teddy, my little brown dog, and headed for the widow's store. It took me a while to get there. I was kicking a can along, and I stopped once or twice to investigate a bottle cap and to pick up a stick to clatter down the neighbors' fences.

I ran up the steps into the widow's store, a living room turned into a grocery, selected two bottles of milk, and went to the front desk, where the widow woman waited, pencil and pad in hand to total my purchases. But when I reached into my pocket to fish out the five-dollar bill, my heart stopped. I rummaged in the left-hand pocket, the back pockets, and my shirt pocket. It was gone.

"I've lost the money!" I wailed. Leaving the milk behind, I ran back as fast as I could along the way I had come. Teddy pumped along behind me as I searched frantically everywhere I remembered stopping. It was no use. The five-dollar bill wasn't anywhere to be found. There was nothing to do but go back and tell Mom I had lost her money.

Mom was still in the kitchen cooking when I came in through the back door, closing it ever so softly behind me. Mom took one look at my crestfallen face and immediately knew something was wrong. Her face darkened when I told her what I had done—it was such a large loss to us—but she quickly brightened.

"Come, son, let's pray. We'll ask God to show us where that money is."

She stood there in the kitchen, her hand reaching down to my slender shoulder, and talked to God. "Lord, You know exactly where that five-dollar bill is hiding. Now we ask You to show us. Speak to our minds, please, for You know that we need that money to feed the family this week."

Mom stood and waited with her eyes shut. The lid clattered on top of the simmering beans.

Suddenly Mom's grip tightened on my shoulder. "Loren," she said, her voice a fraction lower, "God just told me the money is under a bush." She quickly ducked out the door, and I ran to catch up.

The day was deepening to dusk as we retraced my path to the store, inspecting every bush and hedge. It was almost too dark to see when Mom stopped and looked down the street toward a thick evergreen shrub. "Let's try that one!" she said excitedly, heading straight for the shrub. We peered underneath, and there, way back at the base of the stubby trunk, lay the crumpled-up five-dollar bill.

Sipping tall glasses of milk with our beans and cornbread that night, Mom and I told Phyllis and Dad (and the baby, too!) about how God had cared for us that day. We didn't think of such experiences as this one in our family as a sort of school in learning to trust God, but that's exactly what they were. This was a rich heritage that I came to appreciate more and more as I grew up.

One February morning, three months after the experience with the lost grocery money, we children learned another principle that was to play a continuing role in our lives. We were sitting around the breakfast table when Dad announced that he was going to have to be away from home for a few days. He gave me instructions, since I was ten years old, to take care of the family while he was gone.

"I'll be in Springfield, Missouri," he said. "That's halfway across the country, but with telephones and all, we won't really be out of touch."

It was through the telephone that we got the bad news. Dad had been stricken with appendicitis. They couldn't operate—peritonitis had probably already set in, and with wartime shortages, there was no penicillin. It was just a matter of time until he would die.

Mom put the telephone back on the wall and announced that we needed to pray—hard! I crawled behind the couch and stayed there, praying for hours. Two days passed, and Dad continued about the same. We had to hear something from God—some word to help us hold on. Then an event took place that I would never forget.

Three days after we learned of Dad's attack, a knock came at the door. I watched as Mother opened the door to the chilly brightness of the February morning. There stood a man from the church. He reminded me of a funeral director I had once seen, with his drawn features and doleful eyes. He stood there looking more sober than usual, fingering his felt hat, acting as if he was afraid to speak something that was on his mind.

"What is it?" Mother demanded, never shy.

"Sister Cunningham," the gaunt man finally blurted, "God gave me a dream of your husband coming home in a coffin!"

My tongue seemed too big for my mouth as I watched my mom's face. She thought for a moment, then she answered him. "Well, sir," Mom's tone was kindly, but she spoke with a very distinct firmness, "I do appreciate your coming here to tell me this. Hard as it is, I promise I will ask God if the dream really is from Him. With something this important, He'll tell me Himself, won't He?"

It was more of a statement than a question, and with that, Mom thanked the gentleman a second time and held open the door. As soon as the man had left, she went to prayer immediately. "Is that You, God? I promise to try to accept this man's words if they are really from You. Just let me know. That's all I ask."

Mother had such a believing relationship with her heavenly Father that she fully expected Him to answer her on such an important issue in a fatherly-like manner with no shadow of doubt. She left it with God and went to bed.

The next morning as we sat down to our breakfast of steaming oatmeal, Mom put Jannie into her highchair, then announced that she had some good news. "I had a dream last night," she said to Phyllis and me.

We fell silent. "Well?"

"In my dream Dad came home, but it was on a train, and he was wearing his pajamas!"

And that's exactly what happened. We received word that Dad had recovered enough to return to California. He had trouble making travel arrangements because of the wartime military priorities, but through friends he managed to get a berth on a Pullman sleeping car. So Dad arrived just as Mom had known he would, on a train, wearing his pajamas. At the station he pulled a pair of trousers over the pajama bottoms. We must have been a sight, walking down the station platform, supporting our still weak, shaky father as he shuffled along in his bedroom slippers. Dad didn't care one bit how he looked. Neither did we. He was home. And he was alive!

Later Mom pointed out an important aspect of guidance to us. "Getting God's leading for someone *else* is tricky," Mom said. "We can hear a confirming voice through another person. But if God has something important to tell you, He will speak to you directly."

With this kind of family inheritance, it was not surprising that I, too, felt the same call to "go into all the world and preach the Gospel." A call, as it turned out, that would require every bit of knowledge about guidance that I possessed.

THREE

The Little Girl Who Changed Our Lives

OFTEN it is only in looking backward that we catch a glimpse of God's gentle humor as He leads us. I had no idea, for instance, that the stiff, poorly delivered ten-minute sermon of a teenage boy would be the subject of my own life for years to come.

That awkward sermon was my own.

I was thirteen years old when we traveled from our new home in West Los Angeles for a reunion with Mom's side of the clan in Springdale, Arkansas. Dad could be with us for only a few days, but Mom stayed on. She and Dad were both ordained now in the Assemblies of God, and my uncle had asked her to hold revival meetings for the youth in his church. (All but one of Mom's relatives were preachers!)

One night after Mom's sermon, I knelt at the simple wooden altar rail in the front of my uncle's church. Suddenly I felt as if I were not there, but somewhere out in the heavens. Before my eyes, written in bold letters, were the words, *Go ye into all the world and preach the Gospel to every creature*.

The Great Commission of Mark 16:15! I opened my eyes, but the words were still there. I closed them again, and the burning words remained.

I had no doubt in my mind that I was being called to preach. Maybe even to be a missionary, since the words before me said go into "all the world."

I got up from my knees and walked past the other worshipers kneeling at the altar and found my mother. I knelt beside her and whispered what had just happened to me. Mom looked at me with a big grin and hugged my shoulders. Even when we got home after the service, she didn't say much that night. It was the next day that she underlined her real feelings about what I had shared with her.

"Come with me, son," Mother said in her usual direct way. We walked down to the center of Springdale and found the shoe store. She walked right up to the salesman and announced, "This young man would like to see a pair of your best shoes."

I looked at her in astonishment. The shoes I had on still had a lot of use yet. I only wore them to school and to church, but never while out playing with my cousins—we went barefoot any chance we could!

Mom looked into my eyes and smiled. "It's to celebrate, Loren. A little something to say how much your dad and I agree with the Bible when it says, 'How beautiful on the mountains are the feet of him who brings Good News.'"

My family was delighted to hear about the call I felt to go and preach the Gospel. "If you are going to preach," Mom said, "there's no time like the present to try out your wings!" My uncle agreed wholeheartedly, and they decided I could take Mom's place at the next Thursday night meeting, which was only a week away.

The thought of getting up in the pulpit and speaking to the browned, sun-wrinkled faces of these Arkansas farmers filled me with a desire to do my very best. I started to pray diligently about that sermon I was to give. For days I asked God to help me find just the right text. The thought came to me, *Preach on the temptations of Christ in the wilderness*—a subject that was to play a very large role for me regarding guidance in my own adventures.

I felt a bit awkward at the thought of standing in front of grown-ups and preaching about temptation. All I knew were the temptings of a thirteen-year-old. They were very individualized, as I suppose all temptations are. Oh, I had the normal sexual stirrings of any young teenager, but they were not unmanageable. And I'd had my share of boys on the corner lot trying to tempt me to smoke cigarettes, but that seemed just plain silly. I told them so and they gave up.

As I prayed during that whole week before my first sermon, I knew that the "other voices" that tried to lure me away were far subtler, like the urge to keep up with the guys. Not only to keep up, but to excel. Nothing wrong with excelling, but if it begins to twist you, then it's a temptation.

And keeping up with what others were doing just to be accepted did tempt me to do things I'd not normally do. Like ride down the center white line of six-lane Olympic Boulevard on my bicycle, cars whizzing by inches away from me and my buddies as we accepted one another's dares. And there were other things I had to do—my light brown hair had to be parted down the side, dipped just right over my forehead, and plastered back with lots of Brylcreem. My jeans had to be rolled up at the bottom, my gabardine shirts had to have their sleeves turned up exactly one roll, and I had to wear those Chippewa boots so esteemed by the fellows—my own pair had come from my earnings delivering newspapers.

But what was God saying to me about all my trying to fit in? Did He care about my riding bikes down center lines of busy boulevards or using Brylcreem or wearing Chippewa boots? Maybe He did, if pleasing my peers became a problem for me as I set out into my own ministry.

So that was my sermon: on testings. It lasted all of ten minutes. When I finished and sat down, Mom had to do some quick thinking to fill in the unused time. After the service the patient farmers were kind enough to compliment me on my preaching, but I suspect they had to do a little confessing about stretching the truth that night when they got home. The main lesson from that experience was that I'd spotted something that possibly was going to be a real problem. What did "belonging" mean to me? What importance did I attach to people's opinions of me, especially if they were people I respected? Somehow I had an inner knowing that those other voices would possibly be a real testing someday.

We were all about to be introduced to the tan-skinned girl who would change our lives.

Frankly I wasn't paying much attention in church that morning just before my fifteenth birthday. I sat on the wooden theater seat in the auditorium of our church in West L.A., listening to Dad's sermon. But, in fact, my mind was miles away—at a certain used car lot. For months I had been saving up my paper route money to buy a car. Not just any car—it had to be a '39 Chevy. As soon as I got it, I was going to paint it metallic blue. I'd strip off the chrome and lower the rear end as everyone else was doing.

Suddenly something in the tone of my dad's voice caught my attention. Dad was talking about an Arab child. He had just returned from his very first trip overseas to the Holy Land, a gift from the men's Bible class. It was the emotion in Dad's voice that alerted me. His usual booming bass was softer, almost cracking with emotion he was trying to control.

"She was just a little ragged Arab girl, sticking her dusty hand out and pleading, '*Baksheesh!*' That's the Arabic word for alms. I'll never forget her face—not for the rest of my life...."

Dad looked down at the wooden pulpit in front of him. He cleared his throat. The child, he said, had come up to him outside a Palestinian refugee camp. She was about eight. She wore a shabby dress, her hair was stringy, and she carried an even younger girl on her hip.

"Our hosts told us not to give to beggars, because it would encourage them, whatever that meant. But I just couldn't turn her away. I reached into my pocket and put some coins in her hand."

Dad stopped, and I thought for a moment that he was going to cry. The entire congregation had become very, very still. Dad went on to say that in his hotel room that same night he had knelt beside his bed to pray. Suddenly the face of the dirty, tanned Palestinian child came before him. He shut his eyes, but she was still there. Again she reached out her hand, but as Dad looked into her pleading eyes, he said it seemed she wasn't begging just for a coin, but for something far deeper. She was reaching out for comfort, encouragement, for love, hope for the future. The Gospel.

I looked down at my expensive Chippewa boots as Dad continued to speak. All our tears were freely flowing now. Dad told us how he lay awake all night in his hotel room, unable to forget the face of this girl. "And I have to tell you something," he said, pulling himself up straighter. "As of that night, I have changed. I want to give the rest of my life to telling people about the needs of our brothers and sisters overseas. I want to get involved in helping.

"World missions," Dad said, "used to be just a couple of words. But no more. From now on missions has a face. It is the face of a child."

My fifteen-year-old heart raced with a new excitement. Dad wasn't the only one who would never be the same. The words I had seen over a year earlier, written in the air before me in my uncle's church in Arkansas, suddenly popped into my mind. *"Go ye into all the world...."*

Maybe there was something I could give right now.

I tried not to think about my car.

From that night on, Dad reversed his priorities at the church. More and more money was earmarked for overseas mission work. Amazingly, as the people turned their pockets inside out, the local bills also were paid—there was a 30 percent increase in our total church income.

Dad did everything with a splash. For weeks he told us about the lives and challenges facing one particular African missionary until he had us all very interested. Then one Sunday he had a brand-new jeep driven right onto the platform of the church. It would go to help the African missionary if we could raise the money.

At last I had the focus I wanted. I committed myself to give the earnings from my paper route for two months—forty dollars—toward the purchase of that jeep. I didn't buy my souped-up Chevy. Instead, I was helping to buy a vehicle that would help a missionary halfway around the world.

Later I got to wondering. Maybe I could still get my car. I persuaded Dad to let me get two extra jobs in addition to my paper route.

Sure enough, with great pride, which I must say my dad shared with me, I finally managed to save enough money that summer of my fifteenth year to buy my first car. It was just what I wanted, too—a '39 Chevy. The poor automobile was already eleven years old and just barely staying alive. Both rear doors were broken. I stripped all the chrome off and with the help of a friend painted it metallic blue.

But something more subtle was stirring inside me—a quiet, insistent voice told me that my life was to be more than cars or keeping up with others. A trip to Mexico over Easter vacation with ten other fellows three years later seemed to clinch it. I was eighteen, as were most of the others. We didn't know much about meeting people from another culture, but we used our high school Spanish to try to give the most important message on earth. Incredibly, about twenty Mexicans said yes, they did want to know Jesus. Some knelt right on the streets to pray. Even with the inglorious way our trip ended—two other guys and I were in the hospital with dysentery—I knew I had stumbled onto a signpost of guidance.

Something was germinating inside me that I didn't quite understand.

That trip to Mexico was probably the reason I decided that I wanted to go to the Assembly of God Bible college in Springfield, Missouri.

So one exciting day in the fall of 1954, when I was nineteen, my sister Phyllis and I (she had decided to go to Central Bible Institute, too) loaded all of our belongings we would need into my car, which by now had been upgraded to a '48 Dodge.

Mom and Dad and ten-year-old Jannie, wearing her saddleshoes, huddled on the sidewalk in front of our home in West L.A., waiting for us to finish loading up. Then the five of us gathered tightly together while Dad prayed for our physical and spiritual safety. There was a good deal of lip biting as we pulled away from the curb.

But as I nosed my car east on Olympic Boulevard, heading for Springfield, Missouri, fifteen hundred miles away, I was about to be launched into an adventure that would take a lifetime to explore.

FOUR ⬦

Waves

IT WAS just a trip to the Bahamas, but a unique experience of guidance there set the course for the rest of my life.

While in school in Missouri, three other young men and I, all about twenty years old, decided to form a gospel singing quartet. Over the holidays we took trips farther from Springfield than we could reach on weekends. One of these trips took us to Nassau, the capital of the Bahama Islands.

It was June 1956, and we were aboard Mackey Airlines on the short hop from Miami to Nassau. Below our prop-driven plane lay a string of islands in the most incredible colored water I had ever seen—broad bands of light aqua, deep turquoise, and lavender.

When the missionary picked us up at the airport and drove down the left side of the road, I found myself intrigued. I had not felt like that since I was eighteen and had gone with the ten others to Mexico. (It was hard to believe that mission trip was already two years ago!) The elation I was feeling came from more than local color, the flowers, or the traffic police with their white tropical suits and pith helmets. It was something stirring inside of me.

Between our singing performances, we talked a lot with the various missionaries who were working in the Bahamas. They told us about an awkward situation on one of the out islands. Three teenagers had come down to do missionary work—totally on their own! They had started dating the island girls, not knowing that in the Bahamas, dating was never casual, as it was in the States. And now the island was full of damaging rumors.

I listened with mixed emotions. I was sorry those teenagers had been culturally insensitive to the local beliefs concerning dating. But in the back of my mind, I thought, *What a neat idea they had. Young people coming here to do missionary work!*

That night after our singing engagement, I returned to the missionary's guest room with its white walls, unadorned except for an island scene in a cheap wooden frame. I lay down on the bed, doubled the pillow under my head, and opened my Bible, routinely asking God to speak into my mind.

What happened next was far from routine.

Suddenly I was looking at a map of the world, only the map was alive and moving! I sat up and shook my head and rubbed my eyes. It was a mental movie. I could see all the continents, and waves were crashing onto their shores. Each wave went onto a continent, then receded, then came up farther until it covered the continent completely.

I caught my breath. Then, as I watched, the scene began to change. The waves became young people—kids my age and even younger—covering all the continents of the globe. They were talking to people on street corners and outside bars. They were going from house to house and preaching the

Gospel. Everywhere they went they were caring for people just as Dad cared for the little girl reaching out for *baksheesh*.

Then just as suddenly as it had come the scene was gone.

Wow! I thought. *What was that?*

I looked where I had seen waves of young people but saw only the white wall of the guest room with the island print in its wooden frame. Had I imagined the vision, or had God shown me the future?

Was that really You, Lord? I wondered, still staring at the wall, amazed. Young people—kids, really—going out as missionaries! What an idea! I thought about the three boys on the our islands and the harm they had unwittingly done by just being normal kids. If this strange picture really had come from God, there must be a way to avoid such cultural problems and yet harness all that youthful energy for world missions.

Why, I thought, *did God give me this vision? Is my future somehow linked to the waves of young people?* For a long time I lay there staring at nothing at all and pondering what I had just seen. One thing was certain. I knew I could tell no one about the vision. Not until I understood what God meant by it.

I started to realize that a pattern was beginning to emerge: God would speak to me and give a distinct call, then a testing would come. When I was a young teenager, God had spoken through the image of that little girl and her call of *baksheesh*. The question was whether I'd try to keep up with the guys with my Chippewa boots and '39 Chevy or hear that call. Now, two days after the strange vision of the waves, came the early stage of a bigger testing. What a paradox that it came as the result of a good turn of events, one that would put me in touch with my family's past.

When we flew back into Miami for our next engagement and checked into a motel, the others wanted me to go out. "Loren, we're ready to go eat. You coming?"

"No, thanks, I think I'll pass."

Long before our plane had touched down, something had been stirring in my mind. A broken family tie was here in Miami that was more important to me right now than a meal with the guys. I knew my aunt Arnette lived here—the one who had disowned Dad twenty-seven years ago when he decided to become a preacher. Over the years other relatives had told us Aunt Arnette had done very well for herself. She now owned a furniture factory and several retail stores in the area. As for the youngest sister, Aunt Sandra, no one seemed to know where she was. I knew from Dad that after all those years, Aunt Arnette was still bitter. Dad had managed to contact her three years ago when Granddad Cunningham died. She had said, "I wouldn't cross the street to come to his funeral."

What will happen if I try to call her? I thought to myself.

As soon as I was alone, I reached into the drawer beside the bed and pulled out the phone book. A shiver of excitement swept over me. There it was—the same name in the phone book. Arnette Cunningham. Could it be my aunt Arnette? I dialed the number.

"Hello?"

Her voice! I had never heard it before, of course, yet it had a familiar timbre—she *sounded* like a Cunningham.

"Hello, I'm Loren Cunningham. My father is Thomas Cecil Cunningham. I wonder if I'm your nephew, and if I could meet you?"

A silence. Then, "No, I can't! I'm too busy!" Click.

The next day was Saturday. My friends were going swimming, and as much as I loved spending time on beaches, I surprised myself by choosing again to stay at the motel. Alone in the room, I stretched out on the bed and looked at the phone. I couldn't forget that brief and terse conversation with my aunt the day before. It had opened a whole closetful of family memories.

I leaned against the headboard of the bed, staring across the little motel room. Through the years, all of our unopened letters had been sent back, and any phone calls had been refused as well. Yet something about the sound of that strange but familiar voice made me want to try once more. I reached for the phone.

"Hello, this is Loren again. I'm sorry to bother you, but tomorrow I'll be leaving town. I wonder if I could meet you?"

"I'm sorry, but my employees are having a birthday party for me today, and I couldn't possibly see you."

Aunt Arnette hung up again, but I'd made an inch of progress. At least she gave an excuse for not seeing me. I got an idea and went shopping.

What do you buy a woman for her birthday when you don't know her? I decided on a linen handkerchief with lots of lace, like Mom always loved. Then I carefully chose a birthday card not too sentimental, but one that said "Happy Birthday, Aunt."

By Sunday noon we were ready to leave town. I called from a phone booth on Biscayne Boulevard, asking her for just a few minutes of her time before I left town. This time Aunt Arnette, perhaps out of sheer curiosity, agreed to see me.

We drove our station wagon through palm-fringed streets where houses sat comfortably amid tropical landscaping. After a few minutes, we finally pulled up before a large gray-blue house with a screened front porch. Remembering Arnette's bitter words, scorning my dad for choosing to "tramp through life, living off charity with religion as an excuse," I hastily checked my hair in the rearview mirror and straightened my tie.

As I got out, leaving my friends to wait in the car, I could see the shadowy outline of a woman watching me from the screened porch. I walked measuredly up to the steps.

Suddenly I was face-to-face with a woman who looked like Dad. She had carefully coifed hair and was wearing large diamonds on her fingers, but strangely, somehow, I felt a sense of belonging.

"Hi, I'm Tom's boy."

Aunt Arnette looked me over slowly, searching my features. A long silence followed as we stood there on the steps.

"I bought you a little something for your birthday," I said at last, handing her the card with the handkerchief tucked inside.

Aunt Arnette took the card. "You look so much like your father!" she said. And then, softly, "…the same brown hair, the same eyes. The same smile. But you're a little taller, aren't you?" There was a heartbeat's pause. She smiled, wavering, then suddenly her eyes filled. "It's been so long…."

Then she urged me to come inside and to bring my friends, too. I thanked her for the kind invitation but told her as I stepped in that I really had only a few minutes. I answered her quick questions about my parents, explaining that I, too, was preparing to be a minister, going to school in Missouri and traveling with the singing group through the summer. We had just come from the Bahamas. She asked how far north we would be going. I told her, and another silence filled the room as her eyes continued to measure me. Then she said carefully, "You have another aunt, you know, Loren. Compared to your aunt Sandra, I'm a pauper."

That was quite a statement, I thought, glancing around me. When Aunt Arnette learned that our tour would take us near Aunt Sandra's summer home, she urged me to contact her.

I looked at my watch. It really was time to go. We shook hands, and she asked how she could find me. I left her a copy of our itinerary.

A few days later, Aunt Arnette called us on our tour to say she'd arranged for me to meet my aunt Sandra. A chauffeur was sent to the Pentecostal church where we were singing to drive me to Aunt Sandra's summer home in Lake Placid, New York.

Aunt Sandra and her husband, George, moved in a glamorous world I had never known before. But what really impressed me was Aunt Sandra herself. It was hard to believe she was fifty, with her laughing gray eyes and wavy, short brown hair. She was kind, too, making me feel totally at ease—reminding me of my sister Phyllis. Aunt Sandra took me in like a long-lost son. Even Uncle George, a tall, cool New Englander, was cordial.

The extent of their acceptance of me was demonstrated before my last year at Central Bible Institute. My parents and I had worried about how we were going to come up with my tuition. But Aunt Sandra wrote to say that they had decided to provide the money for me to continue my education—as far as I cared to go.

The next year, Dad, Arnette, and Sandra were reunited after so many years apart. A happy ending, I smiled to myself. What I didn't see at all was that the reunion had set the stage for a major testing.

FIVE

Small Beginnings

"WELL, son, you're certainly moving fast!" Mom said one day as I searched my closet for a dress shirt. I was twenty-four, and in the three years since returning to California from college, it had been convenient to move back in with my folks, who were living in a hillside house in Monterey Park.

"Yes," I said absently. I wasn't sure that Mom meant her comment as a compliment, but I was glad she had noticed.

"But, son, you need to keep everything on the altar. If you get proud, God won't be able to use you. Remember that."

After Mom left the room, I walked over to the window and looked at the cactus plants outside. My thoughts raced over the last year at school. I had graduated valedictorian of my class and was president of the student body. I had received my ordination as an Assemblies of God minister, and I had a good job as leader of youth activities in the Los Angeles area. I was glad for all that but ... proud? Mom usually hit the mark with blunt accuracy, but this time I felt she had missed it. It would be years before I saw the truth in her words.

Right now I was far more concerned with my restlessness. I felt something was missing. I enjoyed my work—the young people were all so bright and eager. But I had to admit that most of the activities I planned for them were empty. They missed the heart of the young people because they offered no challenge. That's what we all long for, especially in our teens and early twenties. The big challenge.

I remembered again that strange vision I had seen in the Bahamas of waves of young people going all over the world. Had it already been four years? The contrast between that vision and my little efforts here in L.A. was cruel. I decided it was time to do something to change that.

So a few days later, I went to my district leader with the idea of taking teens on a missionary trip to Hawaii. The plan was approved and we did go. With 106 people! We had mixed results, though—half of them only wanted to be on the beaches; the other half wanted to talk to people about their faith. *You can't mix purposes, Loren,* I said to myself after that trip.

Odd! I found that I was tucking away certain experiences, making a mental list. One: From the three boys in the Bahamas (who had caused such a stir dating local girls) I saw that once on a mission, dating was out. Two: From Hawaii I learned that you can't mix sightseeing with the single-minded purpose of evangelism.

Why was I making notes to myself about what I had observed? And why was I returning so often to that vision of the waves that I had seen in the Bahamas? That unusual memory just wouldn't go away. It seemed to spoil me for the ordinary activities of life. Eternal issues were at stake, and I had to be a part of that Great Commission.

I had to find out what that experience meant and what God wanted me to do with it. Maybe the best way would be to go out by myself for a while to scout out the possibilities of evangelism overseas. My travel agent got me a super-discounted around-the-world ticket. I sold my car to raise the money, took a leave of absence from my job as youth director, and set out to see a world that was in trouble and in desperate need of Jesus. From the very first country I visited, I knew I was not on this trip just for sightseeing. I did enjoy all the new experiences, but I had a strange certainty that I was being guided toward something I could not yet see. Something beyond what I could even think of.

As I traveled through country after country, what hit me the hardest was that people are people everywhere. We are just enclosed by different "systems" that separate us. In India the fact that millions had utterly different beliefs from my own took on a gut reality in an experience in an isolated village.

It was a dark, hot night, and I was returning to my hotel room when I heard an unearthly wail coming from a crowd and decided to investigate. Making my way to the middle of the commotion, I saw a huge pile of sticks. A man with a torch put the sticks afire, and by the growing light, I saw on top of the pyre some thin legs and a still boyish frame. I learned from someone who spoke English that the sixteen-year-old boy had been killed in a knife fight. The wailing reached a feverish pitch, and as I stood there with the people in the flickering firelight, I was overcome with the realization that this boy had gone out into the void of eternity without Christ. A heavy, unrelieved despair hung in the air, mixed with the sick sweet smell of burning flesh.

I would never forget the hopelessness I saw in that group gathered around the pyre in inconsolable grief. I was left with an overwhelming desire. I wanted to be able to say to those who were still alive: There is hope, and His name is Jesus.

As I left that village and continued on through India, that image indelibly burned into my mind. I also sensed that another change was happening to me on that trip. Something of a far more personal nature.

Though I was a part of a loving and supporting family, for the first time I began to feel terribly alone, incomplete. I had dated a lot of young women during my college days in Springfield and through my days working on my master's at the University of Southern California. But these friendships, even though some of them were quite serious, never led anywhere.

And now, suddenly, I felt that I was missing an essential part of life. Why was I scouting out here all alone? It hit me hardest when I visited the magnificent Taj Mahal. As I walked through the ornate keyhole arches, I gasped. There, reflected perfectly in the huge rectangular pool, gleaming in the white-hot Indian sun, stood the massive alabaster monument. And all of this magnificent architectural beauty was done by a man for the love of a woman.

I felt so alone as I walked through the archway. I wanted to say to someone, "Isn't that beautiful!" But no one was there.

What am I doing here all alone? I thought again as I walked beside the giant reflecting pool, seeing my lone image looking back. *Why don't I have someone to share with—not only beauty, like the Taj Mahal, but dreams, too, of being able to bring hope to people who needed it?* I thought of the parents wailing as their son was sent into an eternity void of hope. And I thought of all the beggars' hands reaching out to me everywhere I went. Just as Dad had done, I'd dug into my pockets and put coins into as many hands as possible, but there were always more hands still empty. The depths of poverty I saw in India were overwhelming. Somehow I wanted to say to a partner, "There must be a way to help these people, to meet their heart needs and their physical needs, too."

But where would I find a woman who'd understand that, as well as the vision of the waves of young people going out as missionaries? Who would tramp around the world with me trying to find out if the vision really came from the Lord? She'd certainly need to have (as Mom would put it) a "calling" of her own. And, thinking about Mom, who would be bold enough to fit in with my family, all so individualistic and spicy and strong? *Especially Mom*, I smiled to myself!

Finally I returned to my folks' home in California. I began (alone again, and painfully aware of it) to travel around the country, describing what I had experienced on my world tour. I was especially interested in telling young people about the primitive, not so clean and comfortable world that was out there teeming with opportunities to do something important. When it came to telling them just *what* they could do, though, I was a little vague, because it still wasn't clear to me.

I met Dallas and Larry a month after I got back from my trip while speaking at their church in Bakersfield, California.

Dallas Moore, twenty-one, had a square-jawed face, with twinkling blue eyes, brown crewcut, and the build of a football player. He and a friend, Larry Hendricks, also twenty-one, took me out for a sandwich at Stan's Restaurant. Both young men, I learned, were heavy equipment operators, running bulldozers, backhoes, and cranes.

But as we drove toward Stan's Restaurant, we did not talk about heavy equipment. The topic of discussion was cars. Dallas's own car was one you noticed—a '56 two-toned aqua and white Bel Air Chevrolet, squeaky clean (there was not a fingerprint on the chrome) with white tuck-and-roll upholstery. I was remembering my '39 Chevy, and I realized how important my car had seemed to me ten years ago.

But something was wrong. As they talked about twin cams, dual manifolds, and triple carburetors, I just wasn't *with* the conversation. I just couldn't get that excited about cars anymore. When we got to the restaurant, we slid into a booth at Stan's, and the waitress brought our water and left.

I lifted my glass. Cold. Clean. No fear of bacteria here. I looked around me at the other cozy booths, filled with people happily devouring mounds of hamburgers and French fries. Dallas and Larry did not notice my sudden silence. Everyone in the place seemed to be enclosed in a giant isolation bubble—laughing, having a good time while the world outside was filled with those crowds with outstretched beggars' hands.

It was too much. Abruptly I changed the conversation. I began to tell Dallas and Larry about my trip. It all spilled out. The beggars. The sixteen-year-old burning on the funeral pyre. The hopelessness and the wailing. I looked at Dallas and Larry and saw a glint in their eyes—they were seeing it all through me.

"And the really great thing is, guys, there's so much you can do to make a difference out there!" I said.

They were agreeing with me, but then came the inevitable question. "Yeah, Loren, we would like to help. But how could we? We aren't missionaries. We drive bulldozers."

Yes, that was the question. How?

A month after talking to Dallas and Larry, I was driving down Pacific Coast Highway toward L.A. with some friends, Bob and Lorraine Theetge. Bob, a tall, still-boyish forty-year-old, was a businessman. He and his pert, black-eyed wife were part of a church where I had worked in Inglewood.

As we hummed down the highway, with the waves crashing onto the beach just feet away, I began to think of my dilemma.

Everywhere I went, I met young people like Dallas and Larry who were ready...*eager*...to do something important.

One young man had written on a card, "I'm ready to die for Jesus!" I held that card in my hand and suddenly saw what I had been doing wrong. I had been telling young people to give their lives away, yet the present system required years of schooling first. By that time most would have forgotten their fiery zeal. I was all for education and was working on my own master's at USC, but I'd had strong motivations that propelled me through school without losing sight of my calling.

I knew I could no longer challenge young people when there was no channel for them. I looked out the car window at the surf rolling in and remembered the vision. It was time to do something, but what?

"Loren, you're a million miles away!" Lorraine said, grinning at me from the front seat.

"At least a few thousand miles," I admitted. "I've been thinking…about kids, and how they want to do something for God that really counts." I began to tell Bob and Lorraine about the shocking needs in the world and what I saw as the wasted resources of youthful energy.

As I spoke I found myself referring to the mental notes I'd been making. I explained how we should recruit young people and send them out right after high school so that later when they went to college they would have a new and deeper purpose. We'd send them for short periods of missionary service— a couple of months or a year. Everyone would know he or she was there for evangelistic work, not sightseeing. Each would pay his own way. (No one would be along for a free ride to see the world.)

One more idea sprang out big in my mind. It was new, but it had that ring of certainty: Whatever missionary work we did, we should be open to volunteers from all churches, not just one denomination. I was astonished to see how clear my thinking had become.

And then Bob said three little words. He turned toward me and said quietly, "Let's do it!"

I knew in that instant that something exciting and wonderful had begun.

Bob didn't say, "*You* do it." He said, "*Let's* do it!"

Sometimes God speaks spectacularly, I thought to myself, as with the vision of the waves in the Bahamas. But just now, He had spoken through three words from a friend: Let's do it!

We decided on a name and started Youth With A Mission in December 1960. We set about looking for our first volunteers. Needing someplace to meet with recruits, I turned my bedroom at my folks' house into an office. "I can help you get a Naugahyde sofa bed, Loren," Lorraine suggested. "That'll give you room for a desk."

Soon Bob and I were lugging a brown sofabed into my bedroom-turned-office. With one typewriter and a used mimeograph machine, which we set up in my parents' garage, we began printing our first announcements to send to a list of pastors for distribution to their young people.

I enlisted Mom, Dad, and Jannie, now a high schooler, to help fold, address, and stamp the 180 just-dried announcements. We worked on the living room floor by the big windows looking out over the San Gabriel Valley. My sister Phyllis escaped the chore because she now had a home of her own, having married Navy Lieutenant Leonard Griswold. They were both teaching school in Los Angeles, and Phyllis was expecting their first child in January.

"Hey, big brother, how come I'm not getting paid for this?" Jannie asked.

"You'll get your reward in heaven, sis!" I laughed. But I thought again about the conditions we were laying out in the papers we were folding. We were calling people to serve without pay—in fact, they would be paying their own way to go! Rugged evangelism, not sightseeing. And no dating.

When I carefully placed the bundles of newsletters in front of our local postmaster, I imagined the response we'd get back from everyone. "Where has this idea been?" they'd all say. "This is great!"

The reaction wasn't long in coming, but it was hardly what I had expected. Oh, the kids were excited. Already we were getting letters back from potential volunteers. It was Dad who alerted me to the fact that some leaders were less than enthusiastic about my idea. (By now, Dad was no longer pastoring a church, for he had been elected as a local official in our denomination—with a special portfolio for missions.) I decided to go to Springfield and speak to those in charge of missions.

The leaders were cordial enough to me, a young greenhorn, but they pointed out all the inherent problems in my plan. Inexperienced young people would be an explosive element overseas, they explained. With rising nationalism and political unrest, the denomination had its hands full keeping the *experienced* missionaries from getting kicked out. They pointed out that the complexities of different cultures presented another set of challenges. And there were real dangers and diseases. The last thing they needed was a bunch of thrill-seeking kids complicating the worthwhile job the real missionaries were trying to do.

One of the men must have seen me wilting, because he leaned forward and made a counter proposal.

"Now, if you were to send out *vocational volunteers*, Loren—say to some really well-established compounds where they could be properly supervised," he paused, letting this idea sink in, "why, if you were to do that, I'd stand on a chair and cheer you on!"

Why not? I thought.

As soon as I returned to California, I learned about a great opportunity in Liberia for some heavy equipment operators to build a road through the jungle to a leper colony. I immediately thought of Dallas Moore and Larry Hendricks. I called Dallas in Bakersfield and explained how he and Larry could be our very first volunteers. When he asked about money, I explained that they'd be responsible for their own funding. Dallas said he'd talk to his folks and to Larry, and I waited several anxious days for their reply.

Finally Dallas called me back. I held my breath while he began in his slow way to tell how they had talked it over with their pastors and their folks, and...well...they felt it was right.

Great! I shouted inside. *It's actually starting!*

Then Dallas added one more thing. "And as for the money, Loren. Well, I'm selling my Chevy."

Lorraine Theetge continued to work every day without salary, as did all of us. (My own income came from occasional offerings given to me at speaking dates.) By now we had a nickname among ourselves for Youth With A Mission—we called it "YWAM" (rhymes with "I am"), and the volunteers were "YWAMers."

Before Dallas and Larry finished their preparations to leave for the leper colony in Liberia, we had several more YWAMers getting ready to go to other mission posts.

I was so busy scouting out possibilities for new recruits that I was in Nigeria when Dallas and Larry headed off for their year in Liberia that October. Dad told me in a letter that they had a great send-off. Dad and others had clustered around the two boys in the L.A. airport, laid their hands on them, and prayed for them. Then Dallas and Larry boarded the 707 TWA jet for Liberia.

Fantastic! I thought as I refolded the letter. The first two YWAMers were on their way. It wasn't waves yet, but it was a beginning. Somehow I knew inside that thousands more would soon be going out like Dallas and Larry.

Back in the United States, I made plans to spend a day with Aunt Sandra. She and Uncle George had asked me to visit them. She said they had something they wanted to talk to me about. I was sure they were going to offer me a job—a very good job. I called Aunt Sandra and told her I could come by during my trip.

And so it was that I had found myself once more welcomed into the comfortable world of George and Sandra Meehan.

I twisted in the silk sheets and peered out at the sky. I had not fallen asleep until very late, and now the sun was high, bathing the elegant bedroom in a brilliant whiteness. Today Aunt Sandra was no doubt going to offer me that job, and I'd have to tell her I'd heard the voice of God telling me to take another path. Refusing her generous offer was going to be difficult. They had been very kind in helping me finish my education. The question was, Would I continue to obey God's guidance for my life? I traced my finger over the monogram on Aunt Sandra's silk sheets. I certainly did enjoy the nicer things that money could buy. Ever since I'd worked so hard on my paper route to get myself some Chippewa boots and a Chevy with metallic blue paint, I had had an appreciation for quality things. It was a good feeling being here in these affluent surroundings, riding in Aunt Sandra's Cadillac— even driving it occasionally

I looked at my watch. Nine o'clock! I rang for Hawkins, who appeared in minutes bearing a breakfast tray with all my favorites—ripe melon, waffles, eggs, bacon, and a tall glass of fresh-squeezed orange juice.

I hurriedly ate and went downstairs. Uncle George had already left, but I went through the French doors in the back of the house to find my aunt waiting for me on the terrace. She stood and greeted me with a cool kiss on my cheek. Gail, the boxer, was circling my legs, licking my hands.

"Loren! Good morning, dear! How did you sleep?"

"Fine," I said halfheartedly, "just a little long, I'm afraid!" We went over to the lawn furniture and sat down.

"Loren, we're so glad you were able to come by. I've… we've been anxious to know if you would consider coming to work with Uncle George."

Here it was! The question I knew I had to answer, the moment I had come here to face. I really cared for this woman, and I understood all too well the generosity of Uncle George's invitation. What they were offering was a chance to become part of their multimillion-dollar family business—like a son, an heir. It was ironic that I was facing the same temptation my dad had faced so many years before when Arnette had generously tried to help him with his education.

Now here I was a generation later facing the same test from another of my father's sisters. And the fact that I cared so much for her made it all the harder to do what I knew I had to do.

"Let's go for a walk," I said, stalling.

Gail jumped up and ran ahead of us as we strolled across the expanse of lawn toward the sea wall and Lake Worth that lapped at the back of their property. We stood together, looking across the broad body of water. I took a deep breath.

"It isn't that I don't marvel at what you've offered me, Aunt Sandra."

"But you're saying no, is that it?"

I tried to describe—not explain, for I couldn't—how I had heard that call to preach years ago when I was thirteen. I told

her how, when I was twenty, God had spoken again by show-
ing me that vision of waves of young people taking His Good
News to every continent of the world. Somehow, as I heard my
voice telling her about my vision, it sounded presumptuous.

"I've heard all this, Loren," Aunt Sandra said, her voice
soft but a little edgy. "But at least, couldn't you just do your
work in the United States? There are plenty of people right
here who need help."

*And think of all the help you could give them if you had thou-
sands of dollars at your disposal*, a voice said inside me.

I looked at Aunt Sandra's face, saw the worry and concern,
and a knife twisted inside me. I hated letting her down, but
I knew I had to put this test behind me. I found my voice.

"I can't, Aunt Sandra. I just cannot. It's to the whole world
that God has called me, and I have to obey Him."

Aunt Sandra turned and took both of my hands. "Loren,
Loren. Our family has been torn apart too much already by
religion. Let's not have it happen again. Good luck in your
work. And give my love to your mom and dad. I'll explain to
Uncle George. As best I can, I'll explain."

It was over. I walked through the big double doors and
down the wide marble stairs, hearing Hawkins closing the
doors firmly behind me. I turned once and caught a glimpse
of Aunt Sandra at the library window.

I determined as my taxi drove me away from the Meehan
home that I was going to stay close to Aunt Sandra and Aunt
Arnette. But no matter what, I would stay true to my calling.
As we drove over the bridge toward the airport, I wondered
about my next step and the waves. *Waves?* We now had six
volunteers out or on their way. That hardly seemed like the
thundering waves God had shown me that day in the
Bahamas. It was merely a trickle.

SIX

Helpmate, Wife, and Friend

HOW could I have ever guessed that the young woman in the frumpy dress would be so important to me?

It was two years since we had started YWAM, and I was riding with some new friends, Ed and Enid Scratch, and their daughter, Darlene, to a lunch date in the San Francisco Bay area. The blond girl (I guessed she was in her early twenties) sat on the far side of the back seat. She was quiet almost to the point of seeming hostile. Her dress was so drab—some black-and-brown-checked thing. I had met lots of girls in my twenty-seven years, and I figured this one must be very conservative.

Again and again, though, I found my eyes wandering over to Darlene. She would never look at me, but she wouldn't initiate conversation with her parents, either, as if some small tension lay between them. She did have pretty honey-colored hair, and she certainly filled out that nondescript outfit nicely.

"They have a great smorgasbord at this restaurant, Loren," Darlene's father said, filling an awkward silence as we drove up to Dinah's Shack. And he was right. We all made our way down the long serving tables groaning under a delicious array of entrées. We settled down to our meal with short bits of conversation interrupting long stretches of uncomfortable silence.

"What is this Youth With A Mission?" Darlene asked abruptly, her blue eyes looking straight at me.

"Uh, well, I...that is we...want to see waves of young people going out all over the world as missionaries." I didn't have a lot more to report, actually. Dad had recently visited Dallas and Larry in Liberia. They were doing great, building their jungle road to the leper colony as well as going to remote villages and telling people about the great God who made us all. I explained to Darlene the vocational volunteer program, the opportunities for kids to help the regular missionaries with their skills. To my surprise, Darlene suddenly became more attentive.

"How many volunteers have you sent out so far?" she asked.

"Ten." When I said it, I found I'd dropped my voice. The number sounded pitifully small compared to the picture of waves I had just tried to explain. And I was still working out of my suitcase. But I did have a staff of two now! Lorraine Theetge had an elderly woman named Mrs. Overton helping her. YWAM consisted of two staffers and a handful of volunteers. Not very impressive.

"Well, I think it's a great idea, don't you, dear?" Darlene's mother asked her husband, rescuing me.

Darlene's father agreed a bit too enthusiastically, then went to pay the bill. The four of us drove back to Ed Scratch's church, where only my olive VW bug and one other car were left in the parking lot. The other vehicle was a black '39 Ford hot rod with a lowered front. "Whose car is that?" I asked Darlene, pointing out the window of her father's car.

"It's mine!" Darlene said. "It's not a Thunderbird, so I call it Thunder*goose*!"

Hmmm. This girl was not as mousy as I thought. I got out of her parents' car and went around to open the rear door. I noticed, as I did so, that Darlene grabbed a quick glance in the rearview mirror and fluffed her hair with her fingers. Getting out, she accidentally brushed against me, and I didn't mind a bit.

Darlene seemed in no hurry to leave after her parents drove away. We leaned against her rakish black Ford and talked into the afternoon. It was one of those perfect California days with a light breeze coming in from the Pacific. I learned that Darlene had a fulfilling job as a registered nurse.

Darlene herself came from a long line of preachers and missionaries in the Assemblies of God. When I said that I hoped to see a thousand young people preaching the Gospel in the mission field, however, Darlene suddenly became silent.

"You don't think all Christians have a call, do you, Loren?" she asked at last. "Everybody can't be a preacher."

"Everybody can't be a preacher, but every Christian does have a call of his own." I paused. Something prompted me to add, "Or *her* own, Darlene. You have to obey that call—no matter who tries to get you off the track."

Another silence followed. Somewhere down the street I could hear kids shouting in a neighborhood ballgame. I was afraid I had offended this girl, and surprisingly, I hoped that I hadn't. Finally she spoke—and with a grin.

"You're absolutely right, Cunningham!"

I liked her. No coyness, no cat-and-mouse games. Why was I suddenly remembering the Taj Mahal?

I was glad to be back in Southern California in time to meet Dallas and Larry as they flew in from their year in Liberia. I got their story as we drove along. Dallas's square face shone with excitement as he told me about building the road through the jungle to the leper colony and about their week-end evangelistic work. The adventure, he said, was the most important event that had happened in his life.

I said good-bye, knowing that no matter what Dallas and Larry did after this, they would carry with them an extra dimension—a knowledge that they had played a vital part in taking the Gospel to all the world. But even as we rounded off this experience with our first volunteers, I was aware of the incredible size of the task that lay ahead of us.

As I drove home, I remembered an unsettling experience I had had on my early scouting trip to Africa before sending Dallas and Larry out to work in Liberia. I'd visited a village where I was the very first person to bring the message of Jesus. The old chief had nodded his assent when I told him through an interpreter that God had given His Son for the world. I watched as the chief and others weighed their decisions about what I had said.

A few weeks later, I boarded a plane to leave the Congo. I looked out the porthole and saw a thin column of smoke rising into the sky—an evening fire coming from a village just like the one I had visited. Then I saw two, three, then more fires. Everywhere on the horizon, the smoke of village fires was ascending. The enormity of what Jesus had told us to do—go into all the world and preach the Gospel to *every* creature—hit me as it was graphically portrayed below my plane, etched into my mind by hundreds of village fires glowing in the sky's twilight.

Dallas and Larry were back in Bakersfield. I was on the road again, and yet I still found myself remembering the girl in the dull dress. I called Darlene and found her friendly enough, but I sensed she was still holding back. Later, I called again and wrote her, but we could never seem to find a way to get together. Finally I decided on a different tack. I learned that Darlene had canceled a plan to come to L.A. to see her aunt.

"Darlene," I said on the phone, "I want to see you. PSA has a flight leaving San Francisco this Friday at eight o'clock. I will be waiting for you at the L.A. airport. If you're not on board, I will fly to where you are."

Which is how we came to have our first proper date a few days later. Darlene was lovely in a yellow suit, with every blond hair in place. Her manner, though, was still quite reserved. I was off balance, enjoying her company but wondering what she was keeping from me.

On our fourth date, I drove Darlene in my VW bug up to a summit that offered a panoramic view of Los Angeles. The lights of the city glittered in the evening like jewels on black velvet. Darlene was primly trying to hug the far side of my VW.

"Dar," I began, using her nickname, "is there something you need to tell me?"

She looked at me directly and said, "You're a good friend, Loren. You really are...."

"You're about to say 'but.' But *what*?"

"Loren, you were really right when you told me that I shouldn't let *anyone* stand in the way of obeying God. There was someone." (My heart perked at the little word *was*.) "His name was Joe."

Slowly the story unfolded as Dar stared at the gleaming city lights down below. She told me that when she was nine years old she had a vision of herself surrounded by Asian children. Her heart told her it was a call: She was to be a missionary. But fourteen years had passed, and she had fallen in love with Joe, who was not at all interested in missions. Unknown to her parents, Dar was considering marrying Joe, pushing her call to the back of her mind.

"My folks felt something was wrong and were worried about me. That's why Dad twisted my arm into going with them to Dinah's Shack that day. They were hoping I'd meet someone to get my mind off Joe. I was so mad I decided to do the minimum—just be polite. And I wore my ugliest dress!"

I chuckled. She smiled and went on. My comment that day about obeying God's call convinced her that she had to stop fooling herself. That same night, she got down on her knees and gave up Joe.

"I told God I'd obey Him whatever the cost! I'd be an old-maid missionary if He wanted." I started to interrupt her, but she continued. "I asked God just to take away my love for Joe." The next day an amazing thing happened. Joe called her, demanding to know what happened at 10:30 the night before. He said that at that time he suddenly knew he had lost her.

"But, Dar," I said, when she stopped talking, "there's one thing wrong. Did God actually tell you to be an old-maid missionary, or did you add that part?"

Her silence told me I had hit the mark. She had thought that for her, serving God as a missionary would preclude marriage. Now I knew why she had been friendly but had kept a careful distance.

There was one more thing I had to find out about this woman. I knew now that she and I both had a definite call to missions. And her spunk and cheerfulness told me she might even handle living out of a suitcase with me. But could she mesh gears with my family? Especially with Mom?

At our next meeting I drove Dar to my folks' home—the same one where my bedroom had become our first YWAM office two years before. As we walked past the cactus and yucca plants to the front door, I found myself wondering how this first meeting would go. Would Dar see that Mom's bark was worse than her bite? Would Mom like her?

Mom and Dad met us at the door, and Dad's large square frame filled the doorway. Mom stood tall, her black eyes frankly looking Dar over from head to toe. "Hello there, young lady!" Dad boomed, offering his big hand. Mom didn't say a thing. I held my breath.

And then...the worst of all possible scenarios happened.

Mom began to feel Dar's shoulders and arms; then she blurted, "You're too bony...and your skirt's too short!"

"I am not and it is not," Darlene responded instantly, not missing a beat. She said it with a grin, too! "How do you do, Mrs. Cunningham?" Darlene was offering her hand, her blue eyes twinkling. A long second stretched out as Mom stood there, cocking her head. Then she threw up her hands, let out a big laugh, and enveloped Dar in a hug. I let my breath out. I had found a woman who could stand up to Mom—and love her, too!

Over the next few weeks Dar and I kept PSA Airlines busy between San Francisco and L.A. Before Christmas, only four months after we met, Darlene and I were in Blum's Restaurant in San Francisco, sitting on white wrought-iron chairs, enjoying a crunch cake.

"Darlene, I'd like to spend the rest of my life with you." She mumbled something and changed the subject. Later I tried again. "I'm serious, Dar. I am asking you to marry me!"

This time she said, "I'll have to think about it!" Then quickly she grinned and said, "I've thought about it. Yes!"

I gathered her into my arms and kissed her. God had given me my partner, and my heart soared with joy!

Three weeks later, on her birthday, January 5, 1963, I gave her a diamond ring. We set the wedding date for June 14—a little over five months away. In the excitement of making plans for a lifetime together, neither Dar nor I knew how soon we would face a major issue and an important aspect of guidance. We'd need to hear clearly from God about the unique ministry He had planned for each of us.

SEVEN

God Will Speak to You Directly

I SQUEEZED in a trip to the Bahamas during Easter, just two months before our wedding day. It would be good to see those turquoise-striped waters again after seven years, but my purpose was to scout out possible locations for a large missions outreach.

For the first time since our mixed-results experiment of taking teenagers to Hawaii three years ago, I wanted to take out another group, a hundred or more, to put into practice what I had seen in the "waves vision." By now we had recruited twenty vocational volunteers, but I longed for something more dynamic, something closer to what I'd seen in the vision God had given me.

The flower-lined streets of Nassau hadn't changed, nor had the policemen in their white uniforms and pith helmets. As we drove by a beautiful beach, I recalled seeing the continents, the powerful surf covering them, the kids preaching, helping people.

Wouldn't it be just like the Lord to let us have our first big wave right here where He gave me the vision! I thought. I'd long ago noticed that God often gives advance hints of His plans. If we had a hundred kids, I thought, we could possibly reach every home on every one of the thirty out islands of the Bahamas.

The next morning I visited with local leaders from several churches, including my host's church, Evangelistic Temple, a low concrete block building in Nassau, and explained my dream of having a hundred young people come to the Bahamas the following summer for a large outreach. I told them the kids would pay their own way. They'd be here to work, not play; they'd give their entire summer to the evangelistic project. The name would say it all: Summer of Service. We'd give ourselves in service to Jesus.

The immediate response was exactly what I'd hoped for— a hearty invitation. I was excited as I left the church that morning. When I got back home in a few days, I'd be able to tell Dar that we already had our first major YWAM project.

I hurried back to California to my fiancée. We had a classic June wedding in Dar's folks' church. Dar came down the aisle to me, wearing a white silk gown, her blue eyes sparkling under the veil. My dad and Dar's father shared the ceremony, leading us in our wedding vows. My sister Phyllis sang a solo, and her husband, Len, was one of my groomsmen. Jannie lit the candles while Mom beamed from her front-row seat.

Two very special guests were Aunt Arnette and Aunt Sandra. They sat on opposite ends of the serving table at the wedding reception, pouring tea and coffee from silver pitchers. I had a feeling of completion, of a broken circle mended.

"Here, Loren darling," Aunt Sandra said, putting down her coffee pitcher and ladling me some fruit punch. "You have a lovely bride, dear, and I know she'll help you with your work." Aunt Sandra returned to pouring coffee, but I knew that it was all right now—Aunt Sandra was rooting for me *and* my calling, no longer trying to pull me away from it.

In front of the Taj Mahal, I had asked God for a partner—I saw it now as a prayer, though at the time it had been only an unspoken yearning. I was looking for a woman who herself had a call to missions, who could mesh with my crazy lifestyle and with my family. Dar fit the bill in every way. There was one more thing I was eager to discover—how she could find her own role in that calling.

We decided to take a missions trip through Europe and Asia right after our honeymoon to see if Dar would hear from God what her role was to be. We spent a honeymoon weekend in Carmel, California, then stored our wedding gifts in the folks' house. Before leaving for overseas, I took Dar by to see our "nest egg"—a four-bedroom house in La Puente. I'd been able to buy it with a small down payment, finance the rest with Dad as a cosigner, and rent it out to cover the payments. "It'll be a little security for the future," I pointed out to my bride.

Our upcoming Summer of Service in the Bahamas was only a year away, but for now our priority was finding out how to work together as a team. After all, I had been busy doing evangelism for three years now, and this trip was to be Dar's introduction to what lay ahead. The last thing I wanted her to feel like was a tagalong.

Our trip was half over as we stood together before the Taj Mahal. We arrived at a full moon. We stood with our arms around each other, gazing at this huge pearl-like structure gleaming in the blue light. I could really understand as I looked down at Dar, her hair catching the moonlight, why a man would build such an extravagant monument to his wife.

I thought everything was going so well that what happened next took me by surprise. We were in Singapore, living in the small guest room of a mission house built in the days when the British controlled the island. The house had thick walls, high ceilings, creaky fans, bare wooden floors, and square windows with bars.

One day I came in to find Dar lying across the bed. I hurried across the dark wooden floor to her side.

"Dar! Are you sick?" I turned her to me and saw that her eyes were swollen and red from crying. "What's wrong?"

Dar did not answer right away. The old ceiling fan futilely pushed around the hot, humid air. "Nothing," she said. "Nothing really, honey."

Why do women say that, I wondered. "Of course it's something, Dar. Tell me."

A fly buzzed in wide circles above the four-postered bed. In the distance I could hear a Muslim priest calling the faithful to prayer. After a while, bit by bit, Dar finally managed to share with me what was bothering her.

"Honey," Dar said, "I...they all want me to be somebody I'm not." In country after country it seemed, friends had welcomed my new bride and innocently asked her, "Do you play the piano?" "No," Dar had to say. "Do you sing?" "No." "Which Bible school did you go to?" "Saint Francis School of Nursing." "Oh."

"Loren," Dar said, sitting up and dabbing her eyes, "I've been praying that God would do something to my voice—you know how I sound—so that I could sing."

I laughed and assured her that if I had wanted a girl who could sing and play the piano, I would've married one. "Dar," I said, "it sounds as if you want me to tell you what your role is." As I held her hand, I remembered something that kept me from trying to bolster her right now. I recalled myself as a little boy praying desperately behind the couch for my dying daddy, and a man who came to the door with a "vision" about Dad coming home in a coffin, and then Mom's voice saying, "With something this important, God will have to tell me."

I pulled Dar close and steeled myself. Then I held her at arm's length, looking into her blue eyes with the now-red rims.

"Honey, this is something you're going to have to get for yourself directly from God. I'm sorry, but I can't help you."

It was hard to do, but I walked out of the room and left her alone.

Darlene did hear from God for herself. I came back later to find her beaming. "Loren, the Lord has spoken to me from the story of David and Abigail. Abigail said she would wash the feet of her husband's servants. That's my ministry. I'm to be a servant, a footwasher!"

It sounded like so little, especially from a strong woman like Dar, but she was happy, and I couldn't help but be happy for her, too. I held Dar close and thought of what her own word from God really meant. Darlene was the first of many who would be called full time to YWAM, but each individual would have to find his or her own niche. Ministry didn't have to fit some long-held stereotype: God had a unique work for each one. And each person had to hear it from God directly—not just accept my word for what He was saying.

Dar and I both knew that the basic thing was an attitude of heart. Dar had gotten that right. Really right. After Singapore I watched her carrying out her ministry of "footwashing." When she saw a harassed missionary's wife, she'd jump in and do the dishes, insisting the woman spend some time with her children. Dar also shined at making whatever room we stayed in into our "home." She'd pick some wildflowers and stick them in a jar, if nothing else.

And I saw that her serving ministry went in another very important direction. She sensed people's needs and answered their questions, spending time with them one-on-one, hearing them out, planting ideas, giving mature counsel.

I was so glad that God had given me Darlene before this first big project of the Bahamas. The Summer of Service was going to be quite an undertaking. The first big wave of young people would soon be going out. An excitement began to churn in me, and I could hardly wait to get to the Bahamas!

It was a damp, chilly February evening in 1964, several months later, and Dad had a stack of logs crackling in their flagstone fireplace by the big windows overlooking the San Gabriel Valley. Except for Jannie, who was away at college in Springfield, Missouri, the whole family was there, including Phyllis and Len's two children, who were busy playing with blocks in the kitchen.

Dar and I were talking so excitedly even dear Mom didn't have a chance to get a word in edgewise.

"We'll have thirty islands as our target," I said, spreading a map of the Caribbean on the living room floor in front of the fireplace, pointing to a string of dots arcing from Florida toward the Dominican Republic. "We'll try to get to all the out islands with our English-speaking kids and to the Dominican Republic with Spanish-speaking kids. We'll be there two months." (I was glad we'd worked out our dates so that we'd be leaving before the heavy hurricane season.) We would fly from Miami to Nassau on the first of July, just five months from now. From there teams would take mail boats to the out islands. The Summer of Service would cost each participant $160 for two months, including airfare from Miami to Nassau and back.

"That's twenty dollars a week, son," Mother said. "Either this is of the Lord or you're crazy." She tapped her head.

We all laughed, but knowing Mom, she wasn't joking.

Dar and I kept the road hot recruiting more workers for the summer outreach. We went to speak wherever we were invited. "The Summer of Service will be a rugged boot camp of faith," we told young people. "There will be health risks, so you'll have to get approval from your parents and a doctor. You'll also need a recommendation from your pastor. But you'll have a chance to make a big difference in people's lives." We told them they would have to raise the $160 themselves, just as Dar and I were doing, and that it would be all work with no time off for sightseeing, no spending money that would make us "richer" than the islanders. "There won't even be dating while we are on the mission," I said.

The tougher we made the conditions, the more the kids volunteered.

As July 1 drew near, we prayed even harder to be led to the right people. Sometimes our prayers were answered in an unmistakable way. We were in Colorado, and I was speaking to several hundred young people about our trip when I noticed one boy in particular. He was about eighteen. He had stick-straight brown hair and was watching me intently.

I learned later that Dar, who was sitting in the crowd, had heard God tell her to speak to a "boy in a green sweater" about coming on the Summer of Service. As soon as the meeting was over, she made a beeline for the same boy—he was wearing a green sweater. She related to him what God had told her minutes before. The youth was dumbfounded. He kept hitting his chest with his open palm. "Uh, I...I just asked God to have one of you speak to me personally if He wanted me to go!" He fixed a straight gaze at Dar and then grinned.

Dar grabbed his hand, pumping it up and down. "What's your name?" she asked the boy.

"Don. Don Stephens," he said.

I had to wonder what special role this Don Stephens might have with YWAM, given this most unusual way we were introduced to him.

On one of our recruiting trips, Dar and I visited my sister Jannie at Evangel College. Jannie introduced her boyfriend, a slim, wavy-haired Oklahoman named Jimmy Rogers. We sat in our motel room near the college and told Jannie and Jimmy all about Summer of Service. Jannie's response was immediate. "This is just what I've always wanted—something important to do!" Jimmy wasn't as demonstrative, but I could tell by his questions that he was on the hook, too. Good! I liked the young man.

As we got closer to July 1, I suddenly realized Dar and I didn't have the money for our own fees—$320 for the two of us. So I sold our VW bug. We were scrambling now to get all the final preparations done, like buying three used school buses. We planned to use them for the trek from California to Dallas, where we'd pick up more youths, going on to Florida to catch our flight on Mackey Airlines on to the Bahamas.

One week before our flight to Nassau, our three school buses, piled with suitcases and loaded with volunteers, began making their long journey to Florida. Dad called to tell me that at the last minute Phyllis and Len had decided to come along to help us with logistics. "And, son," Dad added, his encouragement and humor coming through the line, "your mother has a word for you again."

"What's that, Dad?"

"She says to remind you that either this is God's idea or you're crazy. And, Loren…"

"Yes, Dad?"

"I agree."

We both laughed. But, in fact, it was a serious observation. We could be out of our minds. On the other hand, it was possible, just possible, that we were unleashing a power that we ourselves scarcely understood.

EIGHT

Blue Waters, Troubled Waters

OUR buses picked up young people as we drove across the country until we had 146 volunteers for the summer—including sixteen Spanish-speaking kids who were headed for the Dominican Republic. From Miami we flew to Nassau. I smiled, looking behind me at our convoy driving down Nassau's spacious boulevards: Kids were crammed into cars and vans, and more were sitting atop suitcases on a flatbed truck. They had responded from many different churches all over North America. We were under way at last.

During the days of orientation at Evangelistic Temple, I saw that two young men were making themselves especially useful. One was Jannie's nineteen-year-old friend Jimmy Rogers, who was already having his style cramped with the no-dating rule, and the other was eighteen-year-old Don Stephens—the green-sweatered kid from Colorado, whose style was cramped in the same way, since his blond girlfriend, Deyon, was with us, too.

I got to know Don right away and liked him a lot. His lithe build showed the toughening of outdoor life on the western slopes of Colorado. He found jobs that needed doing and simply did them without being asked. In Jimmy and Don both, were we looking at young men who would one day grow to be full-time YWAMers?

As soon as the orientation was over, we prepared to move out for eight weeks of evangelistic outreach. We divided into twenty-five all-boy and all-girl teams, averaging six members each, and then shuttled our first group of four boys to the docks to catch the mail boat for one of the out islands. The sun beat down on us as we unloaded the van. Suitcases went aboard the little boat with the peeling paint as it bobbed up and down at its mooring. Then we stowed boxes of literature, a camp stove, and bedrolls on board.

Finally it was time for our YWAMers themselves to climb aboard. One by one the four youths manfully shook my hand, then lumbered across the gangplank to perch atop large stalks of bananas.

"How long will it take for you to get to their island?" I called to the captain.

He wiped his hands on his dirty uniform. "I don't know, *mon*, maybe twenty-four hours if the seas be kind!"

Then they were pulling away, and the guys atop the bananas were laughing and waving. I waved back.

Twenty-four more teams were getting ready to head off— to Andros, where Don Stephens's team was headed; to Long Island, where Jimmy Rogers would lead a group of seventeen; to Eleuthera, where Jannie's team was assigned; to Grand Bahama, where Don Stephens's blond girlfriend was leading a group. We would have six weeks to talk to every person on thirty out islands about Jesus Christ, followed by two weeks visiting homes in Nassau.

After we had shipped off the last team, Dar and I set out to visit as many teams as possible in the Bahamas and Dominican

Republic. In one place, we arrived on our mail boat, clambered up onto the dock, and were met by six exuberant girls. They helped us with our bags and bedrolls and brought us to their "home," an old wooden schoolhouse with windows propped open by sticks. A dusty portrait of Queen Elizabeth primly gazed down on us from above the scratched blackboard.

"How are you gals doing?" Dar asked. "Great," they replied. They had already gone to almost every home on the cay and were especially excited about the young people who were coming to their nightly open-air meetings in front of the store. "It's the only place with a generator, so we can have light."

On our next stop we got similar reports. The youths were, in fact, very good evangelists. As we went from island to island, Dar's and my euphoria grew like a bubble. I wanted to remember all the details so I could tell the leaders when I got back to Springfield what God had done through these young people:

- In one place a bartender made his decision to follow Christ and put his bar up for sale.
- An old man with a withered arm stretched his arm out and was healed. The eighteen-year-old who prayed for him was so surprised she fainted.
- A woman who was almost totally blind began to read for the first time in years.
- A man with a painful, stiffened back was bending over and touching his toes, laughing.
- A boys' team hired a wizened fisherman to take them to an island in a small boat even though there was a squall. The boys prayed, and the white-capped water smoothed in front of them. The amazed man ran ahead when they landed, calling people to come hear the young "men of God."

Dar and I went out to the Bahamian homes with the teams to share the Gospel. I remember sitting in one home on a rickety chair, watching as my partner, a teenage boy, prayed with a woman. The cracks in the wall of the shanty were so wide I could look outside to the dusty street. The woman accepted Jesus into her life, which was the whole purpose for our being there. But what excited me almost as much as seeing her come to faith was the light of enthusiasm in the eyes of my teenaged partner as he handed the woman her very first Bible and promised he would pray for her and her family. When we left that shack with the wide cracks in the wall, I knew that neither the woman nor the boy would ever be the same again.

Six weeks flew by and the 130 young people boarded mail boats for their return to Nassau and our final two weeks in the capital city. We were housed in an old Royal Air Force hangar on the outskirts of town. The hangar leaned in disrepair beside the cracked cement runways that had been used during World War II. To the left of the cavernous entrance were rooms for the girls, and the boys were on the right. Dar and I found a place for ourselves that doubled as a small storage room. We lined up the camp stoves, and Jannie and Deyon were soon getting up at five o'clock each morning, organizing the cooking.

As we prepared for our last few days in Nassau, we reviewed the records the kids had been keeping. Some six thousand people had shown their interest in following Christ. Two churches were starting in the out islands as a result of the efforts of the young people. But the best results were given not in statistics but in the variety of experiences in which those kids saw the power of God at work in the lives of the Bahamians.

Like the time when two YWAMers stopped a man who was headed into a bar with his hand in the pocket of his sport coat. The man stood and listened to them, then suddenly broke down and with tears in his eyes gave himself to Jesus. Then he showed the kids what was in his pocket—a gun. He had been headed into the bar to kill his wife. Instead, the YWAMers and the man went into that bar, found the man's wife, and brought her to faith in Christ. The man and his wife began coming to one of the local churches.

Our plan was to hold a citywide rally in Nassau proper just before we flew out for the mainland. We started the meetings, continuing to visit the city's homes too, but with every passing day I wondered if we could finish out the summer. I began to cast worried eyes on the horizon, where ominous clouds were gathering. We had heard reports of tropical depressions that could bring severe weather. Then it began. Every night (always at the end of our rallies!) the skies opened and unleashed torrents of rain. The kids were carted back to the hangar in an open truck. They were drenched, but having a great time, and singing loudly when they weren't sneezing. I was aware of potential danger, even though the kids were blithely unaware. I looked around the ramshackle airplane hangar, now with water pouring through in several places.

What an introduction to evangelism for young people! It was a nightmare, and it was getting worse. On August 22, I heard that the first fully formed hurricane of the season, Cleo, was boiling across the Atlantic. I rushed to the weather bureau and spoke to the man in charge. "Mister," he said, "if there was any way of getting my family out in time, I sure would do so." The storm had smashed through the French West Indies, then Haiti and the Dominican Republic, where all sixteen of our Spanish-speaking YWAMers were safe. (We held a praise session for the news.) It was now in Cuba, and it could be coming straight to Nassau!

I hurried back to evacuate the hangar. We took everyone to the solid, low-lying concrete Evangelistic Temple. The girls filled the basement rooms with air mattresses; the boys slept between the pews of the sanctuary upstairs. Dar and I took over the little office.

And we waited.

Outside, the winds were howling and water was pounding against the tightly shut louvered glass windows. We got together in the sanctuary and began to pray, not so much for ourselves, because we felt safe, but for all the people we'd met in squatters shacks in the slums of Nassau and in the derelict houses teetering in village after village on the out islands. I especially remembered the home where I could look out and see the street through the cracks in the wall.

That night, there in the church with the storm battering the island, I realized that many of us were in danger of not stressing properly one major part of the Gospel message. Jesus told us there were two important things to do. One was to love God with all our hearts, souls, minds, and strength— teaching people to do that is evangelism. The other command was to love our neighbors as ourselves—to take care of people, as much as is in our power to do. These were two sides of the same Gospel: loving God and loving our neighbor. The two should be almost indistinguishable—so linked that it would be hard to tell them apart.

My heart kept pace with the pounding wind and rain. I was sensing a whole new concept in missions taking shape— combining evangelism with acts of mercy.

The next day, two feet of water ran down Bay Street, Nassau's main thoroughfare, but the strength of the storm had missed us. Darlene and I were in our little office-bedroom when a stocky young volunteer came in with a report.

"I just heard on my radio, Loren, that Hurricane Cleo has killed at least 138 people. It has injured hundreds more and left thousands without homes!"

I looked at Dar and knew that she too was thinking of the shantytowns and the people we had met on the primitive out islands. "Let's pray," I suggested. Darlene and I and the young YWAMer bowed our heads and prayed for people who had lost what little they had, those who were without homes, and those who had lost family.

"I just wish there was something we could do," I said. "If we could go in with food, clothing, building supplies—we could even have our guys help rebuild homes. But to handle so many people, so many tons of supplies, we'd need a ship."

Even as I spoke, an idea began to take shape in my mind. It would be a great idea, wouldn't it! A ship for going to places of real need. A ship filled with kids who could help people in practical ways *and* tell them about Jesus as the ultimate answer to their problems.

But it was a pipe dream, wasn't it? Certainly, for now, there was nothing much we could do, since we were leaving. Seeing the overwhelming need and not being able to do anything was extremely frustrating. We helped clean up the church, then packed our bags to return home. But as we did so, I knew something had been planted in my spirit. We Christians needed to reach out, as Jesus did, into the areas of people's lives where they felt they were hurting. All too often we just let this practical expression of God's caring slide by.

Yes, Hurricane Cleo had sowed something in my spirit. I wondered how long it would be before the seed would begin to germinate.

The eight weeks of Summer of Service were over. We put the kids on the plane for Miami. They had done a great job. There had been close calls, but everyone was doing well. Finally it was time for us, too, to go home. We were bone-weary as we drove to the airport, but we knew, really knew, that this whole outreach had been God's idea.

Waves of young people were going out. We had come very close to our goal of seeing every person reached on thirty out islands and many hundreds more contacted in Nassau. I couldn't wait to report to the leaders in Springfield what God had done through these young people.

Dar and I breezed back home, totally unprepared for the cold reception that hit us there.

NINE

The Key to "Releases"

DARLENE and I pulled our VW van away from my folks' house, where we had been living, and headed east toward Springfield. The late November weather was not likely to be good as we drove toward Missouri, but it couldn't be worse than what we'd experienced with Hurricane Cleo.

Dar and I had a lot of mixed emotions as we left my parents' house that morning. We were sad because of news from Aunt Sandra: Just a few days earlier we had learned that she had cancer. We all called back immediately to assure her that we were praying for her. How glad I was that eight years ago I had decided to try to get back in touch with family while on that singing tour in Miami!

On a happier note, we were looking forward to the upcoming visit with the general superintendent of the Assemblies of God, Thomas Zimmerman. I could just imagine his excitement when we outlined to him what we'd been discovering—that the church could, in fact, guide young people into effective evangelistic work. Our dream was actually working! We had opened YWAM to all denominations, but we still wanted to stay within the framework of the Assemblies of God.

We'd driven straight through to Springfield. Darlene was very tired and stayed in the motel room that we'd rented near Jannie's college so that we could visit with Jannie and Jimmy later. "There'll be plenty of time for getting together with the people at headquarters, honey," Dar said.

So I was alone as I bounded across the marble lobby and pushed the elevator button for the third floor. A few seconds later, I stepped out into the hushed, carpeted executives' domain of the Assemblies of God. These men had known sacrifice in their youth. Many had pastored congregations like the one that met in a blacksmith shop during my parents' early years. So they'd be open to new pioneering ideas for missions. Reports from the Bahamas would have reached them by now. They'd know what a great job the kids had done during the summer outreach.

The secretary ushered me into the superintendent's office. "Hello, Brother Zimmerman...." *Brother* was a special term of respect used in our denomination to underline the fact that we were all brothers and sisters in God's family. Brother Zimmerman shook my hand cordially, then sat down and looked at me across his desk. Indeed he had heard about the Bahamian mission experiment. But if I was expecting a quick endorsement and a blank check to work interdenomination- ally and still maintain my standing as a minister with my church, I was mistaken.

The problem, I gathered as we sat talking quietly, was that new works like ours needed to be brought under the organi- zational umbrella—not outside and autonomous. He said there was a place for me in the Assemblies, but of course I would have to be a full team player. In the end I was offered a job. A good one, too, there at headquarters, complete with a fine salary, a staff, and a budget. "You can continue with your vision, Loren, but you'd be taking out a more manageable number, say ten or twenty young people a year."

My heart dropped to my knees at the very gracious offer he was extending to me. It sounded so reasonable, so secure. Only it was far from what I believed God had told me to do: send out waves of young people from all denominations into evangelism all over the world. I tried to explain what I had felt God was saying to me about what was about to happen. It was much, much bigger than twenty kids a year, and larger than any one denomination. "Sir," I said, "there's another generation coming. It's different from anything we've ever seen."

I floundered, for I could hear how foolish my reasoning sounded. Brother Zimmerman assured me he had worked extensively with young people for decades and knew them well. As he tried to explain his reservations about my plans, I could truly see his dilemma. If I had his responsibility of leading a large movement, I would need submitted people— ready to play by the rules for the good of the whole. But here I was, hearing a different drummer, out of step with my own denomination. That's more or less what Brother Zimmerman said, too. He was sorry, but I'd have to leave the team— resign—if I couldn't play by the rules.

God, is this really You? I said quickly to myself. And I thought I heard the answer that it was indeed His leading. I knew what I had to do. If I was really sure what God was telling me, then I had to obey and accept the consequences. Brother Zimmerman agreed, but he had no choice either.

I shook hands with Brother Zimmerman, thanked him, and walked slowly, dejectedly back to the elevator, back across the marble floor, back out the door, aware even as I left that building that my decision would be forever. I was churning inside, confused about what had just happened.

It was a sober time back in the motel room. Jimmy and Jannie had come over to visit and were shocked when I told them what had happened. As we discussed what had just transpired in Brother Zimmerman's office, the enormity of my decision settled over us.

"People will think I was kicked out," I said.

"And preachers don't usually lose their credentials except for fooling around with women, or getting caught with their hands in the till, or having bad doctrine!" Jannie pointed out.

"What I dread the most is telling my folks," Dar said. My heart dropped a little lower. I looked at Jimmy, leaning forward in his chair, cradling his chin in a hand propped on one knee. I knew he was thinking about his own parents, too.

For a long, quiet moment we just sat there. I was going over again and again in my mind the sobering conversation I had just had with Brother Zimmerman. I clamped my jaw tightly. I was committed not to rebel, but a germ of resentment was settling into my spirit.

Back in California, the word got out that I was no longer a minister with the Assemblies of God. It was difficult for Darlene and me; it was difficult for our families. But I knew that I had done the right thing. Ever since I had preached my first sermon as a thirteen-year-old on testing, I had gone through these challenges. I had turned down the offer of potential wealth from Aunt Sandra, given up my reputation in my denomination, and settled for a risky and presumptuous-sounding call to send out waves of young missionaries throughout the world.

After Jesus was tested in the wilderness, His ministry was released with tremendous power. Now I looked forward to the future. I knew that God would not let us down. It seemed that we were poised on the launch pad, waiting for the liftoff.

One event took place about eight months after our Bahamian experience that had a strange, bittersweet quality about it: Aunt Sandra was dying. I made a special trip back east just to see her after her surgery. When she met me at the Providence airport, it didn't seem possible that she was suffering from a vicious breast cancer. Her face was still beautiful, though paler and thinner, her hair was carefully done, and her hands were faultlessly manicured. She wore a yellow suit, and you couldn't detect the disfigurement of her surgery.

"Loren, darling!" She kissed me on the cheek, then took my arm and showed me to her limousine outside. As we drove along the streets of Providence with the trees bursting with spring green, I brought her up to date, filling her in on our future hopes for YWAM.

"And how are you, Aunt Sandra?" I asked.

Aunt Sandra leaned back. "I've started going to this church, Loren. I'd like you to see it tomorrow, if we have time."

I certainly did. The next day Aunt Sandra and I drove up to a colonial brick Baptist church with columns on the front. We found the big double doors unlocked and went inside to the hushed coolness. A glow from the tall windows bathed the empty pews. Aunt Sandra pointed to the choir loft. "I sing in the choir now, Loren. It helps when I feel I'm doing something for the church."

She had not, I noticed, said she was singing for the Lord. I knew the time had come to do something very important. My aunt was dying, and she was trying to do what was right.

I had to tell her how to receive forgiveness for her sins—how to come to Jesus Christ.

We slipped into one of the back pews, and I just plunged ahead with what was on my heart. "Aunt Sandra, wouldn't you like to make a commitment of your life to Jesus Christ?"

"Oh yes, Loren!" she said, her eyes brimming.

I spoke the phrases of a simple prayer. Aunt Sandra repeated the words after me, giving herself to God and to His care.

"Dear Jesus, I do accept you as my Lord and Savior. Come into my life now and forgive me for my sins."

When I left her later, I somehow knew it would be the last time I would see her in this world.

It was not easy getting back in the swing of our work at YWAM. I often found myself thinking of my aunt. But partly too, I had to confess, I was still feeling off-balance after my visit to Springfield. We were totally on our own now, without the sponsorship of a large denomination. As I looked into the future, I had no way of guessing that the launch pad we'd been looking for would turn out to be located in a tiny country halfway around the earth called New Zealand.

It was January, but it was summertime in the Southern Hemisphere, and the sun beat down as the small seaplane flew toward my destination, a rugged campsite on an island off the coast of New Zealand. I thought back over the past six years since YWAM had started. Twenty-two vocational volunteers had gone out during our first experimental years, then a tangible glimpse of my larger dream was realized when 146 young people went out to the Bahamas and the Dominican Republic. Each year after that, additional volunteers went out during school vacations. The waves were rising very gradually as we sent kids into the West Indies, Samoa, Hawaii, Mexico, and Central America. Yet it still seemed we were missing something.

"Why do we have so few workers?" I asked Darlene before leaving her to come on this trip. Four and a half years after our marriage, we had hundreds of short-term volunteers going out on mission trips each summer, but YWAM had only eight full-time workers besides Dar and me. I yearned to see something I could only call a *releasing*—some tangible evidence that God was really in this dream. Maybe New Zealand would hold the answers.

Now our seaplane circled the sparkling bay, dipping to a rocky inlet on the island off New Zealand, Great Barrier. The remote campsite, curling around the water's edge at the foot of steep, pine-scattered hills, consisted of a few old buildings, a large patched meeting tent, and some smaller sleeping tents. In this camp of Christians, we intended to recruit for an upcoming YWAM outreach in the South Pacific.

Our plane skimmed the water, creating a spectacular spray that obscured my vision. Jannie and Jimmy, Jannie's husband of five months, had come out ahead of me and were waiting for me now at the rocky beach. With them were a couple in their early forties with whom I felt immediately at home. Jim Dawson was an urbane businessman, clad in the camp attire of shorts and sandals. His wife Joy's warm and bubbly patter spilled over as they led me to my accommodations. For my two-week stay, I was given one of the "luxury rooms" in a line of whalers shacks.

About 150 people were at the campsite, and we were telling them about our new idea of taking young people out on mission outreaches. After two weeks here on Great Barrier Island, we planned to have a week of evangelism, visiting homes in a section of the New Zealand city, Auckland. Then we hoped some would join us in the South Pacific region.

I had come as a speaker, but it turned out that I was the one who was learning new ideas on this isolated island. The first came from the New Zealand kids themselves. They had a guidance practice that intrigued me. In their minds they would be "given" a chapter and verse from the Bible without knowing what the reference said; then they would consider whether or not that reading was a special guidance for whatever they were facing. "You'd be surprised how often God uses that as a way to speak," they insisted. The key, they said, was being totally submitted to the Spirit of Jesus; if He wanted to speak, He could use any tool He chose, including this quite mysterious one.

I was in for some other surprises when I was invited to pray with the camp leaders. There were five of us, including the camp director and Jim and Joy Dawson. Four of us were to be speakers, including Joy, but today we were going to pray over the *order* of the speakers. What I expected was a time of general prayer, then a discussion. Instead, one of the people explained to me as a first-timer that in this kind of practical guidance prayer they would ask God to tell each person individually exactly the same thing. I tried to hide my astonishment at what I'd just heard.

Okay, I thought bemusedly, *let's see what happens*.

"Who should be the speaker today, Lord?" the camp director prayed.

I bowed my head along with the others and asked God. I confess that some not-so-spiritual thoughts flitted through my mind. *What if I'm the only one who doesn't hear a thing? Or what if I get some idea that's off the wall?* But the people around me were experienced Christians, and they were all fully expecting God to speak separately, giving each the same answer. So I decided I'd trust God, too. I leaned back in my folding chair, but inside I was on the edge of my seat, waiting to see what would happen.

Then that familiar voice inside my mind said a name—one of the four around me.

"Well," said the camp director, "is everybody ready?"

One by one each of us spoke out the name that had come into his mind. Each of us had heard the same thing! Five different people, yet each had the same answer. A breeze fluttered through an open window, heightening the shiver of excitement I felt inside.

Day after day we found specific guidance in this same way. I was fascinated. The other four leaders had been praying together in this manner for years. Yet I felt we were on the same team. I also had a real sense of belonging.

Then one day our prayer plan didn't seem to work. We were meeting outside so we could soak up the sun while taking care of business. But this time when we prayed, some felt I was to be the speaker. Others believed it was to be Joy Dawson.

I was curious to see what had gone wrong. Obviously someone hadn't heard correctly, I thought.

"Looks like we need to go back to the Lord," Joy stated matter-of-factly. She told us that she and Jim had learned that sometimes this happens, and you need to ask God if there's another factor you don't understand. So we bowed our heads for "Round Two" and asked God for clarification. Then the understanding came to each of us—it was not Loren *or* Joy, but *both*. First Joy, then me. *This really is amazing*, I thought to myself. It was like the Three Wise Men. They each followed the star—their individual perceptions of God's direction—and in doing so came together to be led to Jesus.

It was time to leave for the house-to-house work in Auckland. We had a lot to do to get ready for the special week ahead. I felt myself getting revved up the way I used to feel at exam times in graduate school at USC. And I knew how little time I had for the work I had to do.

I also was still looking for the *releases* we had been praying and waiting for. Perhaps I would learn something in Auckland—some secrets of guidance I did not yet grasp—to bring those releases and to unleash the waves.

Father, I prayed, as our little passenger ferry was leaving Great Barrier Island for the long trip to Auckland, *I'm trying to learn to listen. Please help me see the next step You have in mind.*

An hour later, standing at the rail with the cold spray misting my face, I found myself thinking again of the Bible story I had used for my first sermon. Jesus had been in the wilderness, fasting and praying just before the beginning— the releasing—of His work on earth. I saw a pattern in this story from Jesus' life, but I tried to shrug it off. Could it be that God wanted me to give up food for a while and pray? I opened a door to the idea. "God, do You want me to go on a fast?"

Immediately the answer rushed into my brain. *Yes, and I want you to withdraw from people for seven days. Starting when you arrive.*

I was dumbfounded. With the house-to-house evangelism in Auckland, we had so much to do! "Am I hearing you right, God?" I asked again. Withdrawing from people meant I'd shirk my duties. Jimmy and Jannie would have to do the work of preparing for our outreach, the very thing we'd come thousands of miles to do. "Is that really You?" The only answer I got was another quiet voice saying, *The Dawsons are going to ask you to stay with them. Say yes.*

Well, that invitation was unlikely to come, because the Dawsons knew I planned to stay elsewhere. If it *did* come, I could see God's hand more clearly. I'd know He wanted me to fast and pray. Even if it meant leaving an unfair amount of work on Jimmy and Jannie.

I said nothing about all of this to anyone and just waited to see what would happen. As the boat plowed through the waves, the sea and the sky darkened to evening.

Then, just as the lights of Auckland began to glimmer on the horizon, Jim Dawson joined me at the rail. I held my breath as he began to speak. He seemed hesitant. "Uh, Loren, uh, I know you're planning to stay with other friends, but Joy and I, well, we believe we've heard something from the Lord. Would you stay with us?"

TEN

Coming to God
with a Clean Heart

I GLANCED around the Dawsons' two-story Scandinavian-style home with its breathtaking panorama of the harbor.

Jim ushered me downstairs to their guest room. The room was simply furnished, comfortable, and secluded, with its own outside entrance. I remembered God's words that I was to "withdraw from people." I called Jimmy and Jannie to give them the news that I couldn't help them for a week.

"Well, you have to do what you feel is right, Loren," Jimmy said in his slow Oklahoma drawl. I could imagine his thoughts. *What do you mean we won't see you for seven days? You're going to fast while we do all the work?* But Jimmy said nothing like this. He was too loyal. That made it all the worse.

After I hung up the phone, I knelt on the green carpet beside my bed. Yes, accepting the Dawsons' invitation was exactly what I should be doing. In some as yet unseen way, this time set apart to fast and pray was as important as the work itself. All my life I'd heard about holiness. Well, holiness was probably another way of saying have the right priorities in your life. And for me, this week, getting alone with God was *the* priority. I couldn't help but wonder, too, if this week wasn't directly involved with guidance.

The first two days were uneventful. I would get down on my knees and pray, walk around the room and pray, sit down and pray, stretch full-length on the floor and pray. There was also lots of time for reading my Bible. But most of the time I just waited and listened for what God wanted to say to me. Sometimes God would speak a word or two. At other times, we enjoyed a companionable silence.

It was the third day of the fast before the breakthrough came. The only word I can use to describe what happened to me is surgery. It was like soul surgery.

I was lying facedown on the carpet, waiting on God. Suddenly a sharp scalpel of conscience probed.

"Remember Springfield?"

Faster than I could imagine, displeasing attitudes I had harbored for a long time began to surface. Critical feelings and resentment toward my denominational leaders who hadn't seen the vision of YWAM the way that I did—especially my brother, Thomas Zimmerman. For two years now, since I reported to Springfield after the Bahamas, I'd been smarting under the rejection, and in my heart I'd begun to deny my own roots.

I suddenly saw all the time I had wasted trying to defend myself and my ideas. That time was robbed from the real work that needed to be done—talking to people about Jesus.

As I lay there on the floor before the Lord crying in repentance, I asked for His mercy. From now on I'd speak out in real praise for my former leaders, grateful again for them and for my godly heritage. I'd let God defend the vision, if it was from Him. Lying there on the green carpet, I knew that God had heard me and forgiven me.

The scalpel probed again. And again. Throughout the day, hour after hour. My pride suddenly loomed before me— I saw the times I had acted for the recognition of men rather than God. Mom's words in my bedroom-turned-office a long time ago suddenly dropped into my mind: "Son, if you get proud, God can't use you." Then God put His finger on sins of the mind, sexual fantasies. As each sin—of thought, or attitude, or action—came to my mind, I confessed it, asking God to forgive me and help me to turn away from it.

When I knew the soul surgery was finally over, I sensed in my spirit that I had one more act of repentance to do. I found stationery and a pen and began the first of several letters I knew I had to write in order to make my relationship right with certain people. "Dear Brother Zimmerman...." It was excruciating to have to write and bare my soul, but that night I settled back into bed with a brand-new feeling of cleanness. On my desk in the little room was a tidy pile of letters. The one on top was addressed to Springfield, Missouri.

By the end of the week as I began to come slowly off my fast, I realized that I—and perhaps YWAM—had just passed a turning point common to all who seek to hear the voice of God. We can hear the Lord more clearly if we come to Him with a clean heart. The process of confession was an ongoing one, to be sure. But I'd made a good start. I wondered what would come of it!

The very first event to follow was certainly not good.

Jim Rogers had protected me during my week of prayer, but promptly on the seventh day he called with some bad news. We had shipped one hundred thousand booklets to New Zealand to give out in homes and on the streets. The booklets had arrived during my fast and had been stored in a factory basement. A rainstorm had flooded that basement, and all of our booklets were soaked.

"Could you come right over, Loren?" Jim gave the address.

Half an hour later I made my way down the factory stairs to the damp basement. Jimmy met me and just swept his arms out. Jannie and three other volunteers were pulling thousands of waterlogged booklets out of soggy boxes and stacking them in piles on a huge table.

"I think we can salvage most of them, Loren," Jannie said. She took me to see a huge industrial press. The booklets were placed in the press and much of the water squeezed out. Then, one by one, the booklets were strung on clotheslines to dry. What a beginning to our Auckland effort.

Surprisingly, though, all of our spirits were high. We spent the week drying books on clotheslines, then on Saturday morning we drove to a sleazy downtown address. "Don't you wish Mom could see us now, sis?" I asked Jannie, laughing, as we parked in front of the Pink Pussycat Club. The Christian coffeehouse that we were using as a headquarters was in a basement next door to the Pink Pussycat. We unloaded boxes of almost-dry booklets and took them downstairs to the black-and-red hall, where free coffee and inexpensive sandwiches were served to street people from the neighborhood.

Volunteers in groups of four and five drifted in until thirty people filled the black-and-red room downstairs. I looked at the guys, still in their teens, dressed in popular narrow Continental trousers, and at the girls with their miniskirts and square-toed shoes. My eyes were especially drawn to one teenage guy with a broad Polynesian face and a carefree grin. (Why did he seem to stand out in this group?) Among these thirty young people, could I be looking at future missionaries? Would these same kids someday find themselves in the Philippines or West Africa, or even in countries behind the Iron Curtain?

I took a deep breath and started in, speaking of our reason for coming to Auckland, laying out the plan of action. We were going into Ponsonby, a Polynesian ghetto where thousands of Maoris, Samoans, Tongans, and Cook Islanders lived. Over a map we blocked out a large area enclosing hundreds of homes. Again, the youth with the broad Polynesian face seemed to separate himself from the crowd. He asked bright, pointed questions.

"You couldn't have picked a harder neighborhood," he said.

"I expect you're right. What's your name?"

"Kalafi Moala."

I found I was making note of the name.

Kalafi Moala was right about Ponsonby. It was a tough area. After a cheerless day of almost constant rebuffs, we gathered back at the basement coffeehouse for a debriefing. "I almost caught pneumonia from the draft of doors slamming in my face!" Jannie said.

The next day, Kalafi was my partner. As we walked between rows of once-grand Victorian homes whose gardens were now weed-filled and littered with beer cans, I picked up pieces of information about this young man. Kalafi was eighteen, the eldest son of nine children. Tonga, his home, was a Polynesian monarchy—a tiny archipelago two thousand miles to the east between Fiji and Samoa.

Like most Tongans, Kalafi had been raised to go to church, but there had been no living relationship between him and God. Apparently, he was a natural leader in Tonga's most prestigious school, but he had also been a drinking, carousing troublemaker.

Kalafi went on to say that in the wee hours one morning when he had come home drunk, he suddenly saw the wasteland his life was becoming. He knelt beside his bed and began to cry. He wept for three hours, asking God to come into his life and change him. He got off his knees at eight o'clock a new young man. Kalafi told me how, before he graduated, he and his friends were meeting regularly to pray and read the Bible. Many of the students at his school became Christians.

The first day we had gone into Ponsonby had been almost fruitless. Today was different. When Kalafi, as a Polynesian, spoke to others from the islands, he got through. People listened, especially when he didn't "preach" but just told his own story of God's power to change lives. As the day wore on I began to hope, secretly, that young Kalafi would be part of the release I had been praying for.

I didn't have to wait long. One night in the coffeehouse toward the end of our week, Kalafi said he wanted to talk to me. We found a corner, and above the blare of music, Kalafi came straight to the point.

"Loren, I think we need a YWAM team to come to Tonga." Kalafi told me that next July, five months away, would be the coronation of Tonga's new king, Taufa'ahau Tupou IV. Thousands of Tongans would be pouring into the capital city of Nuku'alofa. "I think it would be an ideal time for your people to be there," Kalafi said.

Then he added, "And I'll work with you—full time. I've decided to give up my plans, and they were pretty good ones, Loren. I'll go back to Tonga instead and make arrangements for the teams."

I looked at Kalafi, suddenly excited. I knew about his excellent career potential and was more than a little awed at what he was sacrificing. This selfless dedication was what we needed if we were ever to grow: young men and women who would hear and obey God's voice for themselves.

"Yes, let's do it!" I said. I knew without a doubt that Kalafi's vision for Tonga was right. That same night, with the walls vibrating from the loud music, we prayed for Tonga.

When I went home to the Dawsons late that night, I thought that possibly Kalafi was our first new leader from the non-Western world. It didn't escape me, either, that he had been released after my days of cleansing and fasting and praying.

My six weeks in New Zealand were over. As I mounted the steps to the plane that would take me to Darlene—we had planned to meet in Hawaii for a second honeymoon—I reflected on how much had happened in this short time. We'd had a successful outreach into a ghetto. And the releasing had begun. Besides Kalafi, there were at least seven others whom I saw as probable future leaders for us. It hit me: eight people! In six weeks' time the number of full-timers in YWAM had possibly doubled.

Even so, we were still adding to our numbers one by one. Someday I envisioned being able to grow not by *addition* but by *multiplication*. Multiplication produced growth so much faster than addition. I thought again of Kalafi. If he were only trained properly, he'd be able to train and send out other young people—especially people from the Third World.

The plane climbed above the clouds and settled in at thirty thousand feet. As the flight headed north to Hawaii, I reflected on all that had happened in my own life these past few weeks. Meeting the Dawsons, the week of fasting and praying, and hearing Kalafi's vision for his homeland was in itself like a training school. I'd been taught guidance principles by people who knew new ways of hearing God. Then I'd put these principles to work. Really, it wasn't much different from growing up in our family. Darlene and I both had had such incredibly rich childhoods of teaching and example from our parents and grandparents that in a way, we had an unfair advantage. Wouldn't it be great to have a school, deliberately designed to be in a family setting, where people could be introduced to these spiritual principles and allowed the chance to try them out for themselves?

What a great idea! Maybe, in fact, it was God's idea! If so, perhaps I could see the Wise Men Principle I'd just learned in New Zealand work in the lives of young people, where two or more people see the same guiding star at the same time. If this idea of a school for teaching the ways of the Lord really came from God, it was reasonable to expect that He'd give it to more than one person. I would tell Darlene about it, of course, but otherwise I thought it wise to keep my next goal for YWAM a secret.

My plane arrived before Darlene's. As I stepped out of the air conditioning of the cabin, I felt that familiar caress of soft, warm air and breathed in the smell of the plumeria trees. I was so glad that we had decided to have this time alone in Hawaii before plunging back into work on the mainland. What was it about Hawaii that felt so right to me? I looked around at the mix of Asian, Polynesian, and Western faces. Hawaii really was a linkage point between East and West.

I had just enough time before Dar's arrival to rent a pink-and-white-striped jeep. If we were going to have a second honeymoon, why not do it right?

Darlene came down the plane steps looking lovely in a blue dress with her blond hair carefully in place. I swept her into my arms in a crushing hug! We threw our suitcases into the jeep and sped away to a small apartment as the wind did a quick job of undoing Dar's careful coiffure.

I quickly brought Dar up to date on all that had happened in New Zealand: meeting the Dawsons and Kalafi, all about the terrible but wonderful spiritual surgery in the Dawsons' home, and especially all the principles I had been learning about guidance. Incredibly, Dar told me that she had been fasting and praying on the same exact days as I and that she, too, had gone through soul surgery. It was amazing to see how God had been leading us together, although we were thousands of miles apart.

We were circling the island one lazy day and had stopped at the Blowhole, past Diamond Head. We parked the jeep and clambered down the black lava rocks. Below us, mammoth waves pounded into the massive boulders, crashing in and then receding. Often a titan would roll in, rushing under some of these boulders, causing a sudden fountain to spurt through a hole in the rocks in a spectacular spray. We sat down on a cliff and watched. The enormous power of the water awed me. Again I pictured the waves of young people and thought how they would need to know how to channel God's power to be effective witnesses for Him.

I had one more special idea I wanted to talk to Dar about, and sitting here by the ocean seemed the perfect place for it, with the surging waves converging beneath our feet.

"You know, Dar," I began, "there's something big on my mind...." And I told her about the school for training young people that I envisioned.

"That's amazing, Loren!" she said. "The Lord has spoken to me about a school, too. So many people have been giving us special input—from the Lord and from their lives—just when we've needed it lately. I'd love to see kids have the same opportunity!"

A mantle of tropical clouds gathered around the shoulders of the green mountains behind us as we excitedly began telling each other all our ideas for the school we hoped to start. The kids would learn how to truly love God with all their hearts, souls, minds, and strength. They would have the chance to learn from special men and women who had been practicing what they were teaching. This floating faculty would come, one at a time, right from the center of action from wherever they were laboring for the Lord around the world.

"And it could be in a family type of setting, with all of us learning together—students and teachers," Dar suggested, reminding me how we had gotten so close with the young people living in the hangar in Nassau.

The kids would learn not only in the classroom but also through practical experience. They would be learning by doing—going to foreign countries, meeting people, seeing the conditions, and helping.

Ideas began to fall over one another. We hammered out details for the school until I noticed the sun was an orange ball, dipping low over the horizon.

Before we left our spot on the cliff, I told Dar about the principle of keeping guidance a secret until God gave permission to share it. Perhaps this would be one of those times when He would show us through someone else that He was in this idea of a school.

We looked forward to a Christmas with the whole family at Mom and Dad's new apartment in Alhambra, California. Jim and Jannie were flying in from the South Pacific, where I had left them ten months earlier. Dad would be busy as usual, overseeing churches and missionaries. Phyllis and her husband, Len, lived with their two children a few blocks away, and it would be great to see them. And, of course, Mom would be there to spark the conversation with plenty of spice.

We walked in the front door of the apartment to the delicious smell of roasting turkey. Mom, flushed from her labors in the kitchen, gave us both a hug, then Dad enveloped us in his big arms, followed in a line by all the others.

I began to pump Jim and Jannie for details about the last ten months down under. I was especially eager to hear about Kalafi and Tonga. There was so much to say, Jim and Jannie were soon vying for the chance to speak. By the time they arrived from New Zealand with their thirty-five volunteers, Kalafi had recruited twenty Tongans to work with them.

People from all the islands had poured into the capital city for the coronation. The YWAMers had given out thousands of tracts. Everyone seemed to want one; nobody threw the tracts away. (I remembered all the refusals in Ponsonby.) Hundreds of Tongans came to know Jesus during the outreach.

"And Kalafi?" I asked.

"He did a great job," Jimmy said.

I thought to myself, *It really worked—it's multiplying now, without my even being there!* Now if Kalafi could only come to our school!

It was nearly time for our Christmas dinner, and Mom was already clanging pots in the kitchen. Dar passed by me and gave me a meaningful look, and I knew she was thinking about the very special package she had slipped under the tree.

After dinner we gathered in the living room to open our presents. Soon the floor was filled with crumpled paper and ribbon.

Only one large package remained under the tree with a tag that read, "To Mom from Loren and Darlene. HOLD UNTIL LAST." As it was placed on Mom's lap, I looked over at Dar—her eyes sparkled.

Mom ripped open the box and with a puzzled look on her face pulled out a tiny Christmas stocking and a note, which she read silently. Her jaw dropped, her eyes widened, and she looked over at us. "Wow! You don't mean it?" gasped Mom with a sly grin.

"What is it, what does it say?" cried the others, almost in unison.

Finally, above the ruckus, Mom read aloud, "This little stocking is for you to fill next year. In July you will be having a third grandchild."

After five years of marriage, Dar and I felt it was the right time to start our family. Everyone started laughing, patting me on the back, and shouting congratulations. Dad sat back in his recliner grinning.

"I'm glad you two finally stayed out of an airplane long enough to get one!" Mom said.

The new baby wasn't the only thing that had been conceived lately. During the fall of 1967, several months after my return from New Zealand, I had gotten the flu. Getting sick was not very unusual, but what happened next was! While I was in bed in California, nursing my aches and fever, a thought came into my mind: *You are to have a school. It is to be called a School of Evangelism.* I wondered if the thought was from God. The idea grew, and I remembered the things Dar and I had talked about in Hawaii. Then another thought suddenly cut through, *Your school is to be in Switzerland.*

Switzerland! *Is this You, God?* I asked in my mind. Sure, I remembered my visit to that lovely alpine country. I had found it entrancing. But why there? We had done nothing in Europe—YWAMers had gone to Africa, the Caribbean, South Pacific, Latin America, and Asia. But Europe?

I told Darlene about it, and we made plans to scout out the possibilities in Switzerland the following spring. We used our "nest egg" house in La Puente as collateral for a loan to get the tickets. I still wondered, though, if this Switzerland idea was really from God. I wanted Him to reassure me that I had, in fact, been hearing from Him.

He did—in a striking way.

Two days before we were to leave, I got an unexpected invitation to breakfast. Dad and his friend Willard Cantelon, a Bible teacher, had made a breakfast appointment. Willard called and insisted that Dad bring me along. "It's important," he said.

Dad and I arrived at Foxey's Restaurant in Glendale to find Willard waiting for us in a horseshoe booth. Willard was dressed nattily in a tweed sport coat, his homburg carefully placed aside. I shook his hand, curious to hear why he had wanted me here.

Even afterward, as I reviewed what he said, I could not believe it.

"Loren, I have a message for you," Willard said. "The Lord has been planting the idea in my mind that someone should start a school in Switzerland. Last night He told me you are to be the one." I found my tongue and mumbled something. Willard went on to say that the school was to have an international student body and visiting teachers. "I'm not to be one of the teachers, Loren. I'm just a channel to pass this message on to you."

As Willard spoke, I found myself getting more and more excited. With this astonishing example of the Wise Men Principle at work, I now knew we were absolutely right in going to Switzerland.

We landed in Geneva in April and drank in the sights of the green valleys surrounding Lake Geneva. Then we loaded into a car and headed for Lausanne. What a sense of anticipation we felt as we sped past tranquil fields, storybook chalets, and immaculate barns!

"Do you think this could ever feel like home?" I asked Dar.

"I love it!" she said. "I could stay here the rest of my life!"

For Dar's sake, we walked around Lausanne slowly, enjoying the flowers, the glitter of Lake Geneva, the twin steeples of the cathedral, and the distant blue outline of the majestic Alps. And all the while we marveled that God had told us to come here to start our School of Evangelism. We made arrangements for a facility in a town outside Lausanne and returned to the States to have our baby.

Dar's time for delivery was close, and I admit that Switzerland was not very much on my mind.

It was July 3, 1968. I was in Philadelphia, and Darlene was in Redwood City, California, with her parents, waiting. The baby wasn't due for three weeks, but when I woke up that July morning, I had a feeling I should call Dar. Her voice was excited.

"How would you like to be a daddy today?"

"Today!" All other business was immediately forgotten. "Are you sure?"

"Yes, I've already gone into labor," Dar said. "My guess is our baby will be born about eight or nine o'clock tonight."

"I'll be right there!" I half shouted and hung up the phone.

But it was easier said than done. I finally got a seat booked on the busy eve of the Fourth of July holiday, only to sit for three hours on the runway of the Philadelphia airport before our plane was allowed to take off. I arrived at the hospital in Redwood City at eleven that night, frustrated and guilty that I hadn't been able to get there sooner.

As I dashed into the hospital, I spotted Darlene's folks in the waiting room. "Am I too late?"

"No," they reassured me, "but Darlene has been having a hard time. The doctor said the baby was coming breech— bottom first."

I rushed into the labor room. Darlene was lying limply on the pillow, alternately bearing down with all her body, then sinking again onto the sweat-dampened sheets.

"I had to wait for you," she gasped, smiling weakly between the sudden grimaces of contractions. I grasped her hand and sat beside her to wait and to pray.

The time came for them to wheel her into the delivery room. Finally, at three o'clock on the morning of the Fourth of July, the doctor breezed in, removing his mask and gloves to shake my hand.

"Congratulations! You have a beautiful baby girl! It was a difficult birth, but your wife was a real trouper!"

We named her Karen Joy. Now we were a real family. And we were looking forward to another birth: the school that seemed to hold so much promise for all the releases we had been longing for.

ELEVEN

Multiplication of Guidance

TWO years had passed since I first glimpsed God's strategy for a short-term school as part of His plan for sending young people out as missionaries. Not many of the kids we met had Dar's and my advantage of growing up in families that were really miniature schools. In our homes we'd learned the ways of God, how He purifies, how He provides, how He guides. God, I now felt, wanted that same experience for all YWAMers, especially those who were to be full-time workers. He showed us this by giving a special leading of the Wise Men Principle. He wanted a family-like school, and it was to be in Switzerland.

It was hard to believe that it had been more than a year since we first came to Switzerland looking for a place to have a school. The past year had been full of experimentation and false starts. The facility we found for our school when we first came proved unsuitable. But just last week a friend spotted an old hotel that was all boarded up. He thought it might be perfect for us, so Dar and I walked over to investigate, pushing fourteen-month-old Karen in her stroller.

And there it was—a big old hotel, five stories tall, made of grayish stucco with old green shutters. It sat on a hill beside a dense evergreen forest. We walked all around the building and then onto the large lawn in front with an arbor of sycamore trees sheltering what must have once been an outdoor café. Across the roof was a weathered, painted sign, "Hotel Golf." ("There must be a golf course nearby," I commented.) We spent some time on the front lawn, enjoying the view of nearby pastures and cows with large bells ("Listen, Loren, you can hear the cowbells!") and, of course, the majestic Alps looming on the horizon.

We found the owner in a two-story annex next to the main building. To our relief she spoke English. She was definitely interested in renting the hotel and said we could see it now. She handed us the keys and told us to go and have a look. "If you need anything, monsieur, please ask. The hotel has been boarded up for years, but everything is there."

Strangely aware that we might often be walking up those same front steps, I turned the key, pushed the stubborn door, and went in. A musty, dank smell met us. Fine cobwebs hung in the corners of the entryway. The lobby was furnished with shabby, though once fine, maroon brocaded chairs and divans. Darlene didn't seem to notice the drabness as much as I did. I could tell she was already making plans on how to fix it up. "We could reupholster the furniture and have a beautiful place, Loren. I can just see kids here, relaxing between classes."

"And look in here!" She put Karen down to crawl around on the faded Oriental rug. A set of French doors led from the lobby into the main dining room. "This would be a perfect classroom." We climbed the wide staircase, exploring all five floors and all thirty-two rooms.

But it was when Darlene found "our" room that I knew she had already moved in. It was on a corner of the second floor and had its own bathroom with a large European-style tub. French windows opened to catch the breeze and let in the music of cowbells.

"So you think this could be home for a while?" I asked, smiling.

"Oh yes!"

I walked through the hotel again, imagining all that could be done here. The purpose of this school would not be to fill minds but to change lives: to increase faith in God and learn of His character and how our character could be like His. Here we would be bonded to the Lord, and in the process we'd be bonded to one another in love. We would learn about the twin nature of the Gospel as I had glimpsed it back in Nassau during Hurricane Cleo. In this rank-smelling building (almost like a stable, I smiled to myself) would be born a school that would see hundreds of kids come to know God in depth and learn how to make Him known to others.

I stepped into the dining room. We'd have the kids for three months in this future classroom, then staff and students would take to the road for six more months of training in the field. Together, we'd trust God to meet our needs. Together, we'd put into practice what had been learned in the classroom, talking to people about the Lord. "These young people will come back with their own visions," I said half aloud. "It'll multiply...."

Dar came in. "Honey, the landlady wants to talk about terms."

"Good. Let's pray about this first." We stood there in the dining room, holding Karen between us, and prayed. We believed God had brought us to this spot, and now we asked Him to bring to birth all we had been seeing for this very special school. As we prayed about the purchase terms and the future of the school, my mind went to Kalafi Moala. I so much wished that he could attend this school. I was uneasy that Kalafi had not been trained or had the opportunity to go to school as Dar and I had.

I felt strongly that Kalafi should be with us to add training to the tremendous zeal he had for spreading the Gospel. He had married a Tongan girl named Tapu. Jimmy and Jannie knew her and reported that she was very pretty. "*And* she's from one of the noble families of Tonga," Jannie added. "They're quite a team!" Still, I was uneasy. Kalafi had a lot of responsibility in his missionary work in New Guinea for someone so young!

But for now my attention was focused on this school in Switzerland and all that was about to take place. We leased the hotel and proceeded with plans for thirty-six young people from five nations to join us for our first School of Evangelism, not quite realizing that we were also about to be launched into another of the most basic lessons in guidance.

Ever since that breakthrough experience in the Dawsons' home in New Zealand, when I experienced such a deep surgery of the soul, I'd known that being transparently honest before God and before man was necessary if we were to make progress hearing God's voice. I'd seen for myself how God's power was released after a time of cleansing, and I remembered that in every great historical move of the Spirit I had studied, every revival had experienced times of confession and deep repentance. I could see why, too. The cleansing season had set me free—the devil had none of my secret resentments and sins to hold over me anymore.

I'd never wanted to press confession with YWAMers, but I wondered if someday others would experience it, too. So what happened with my friend Don Stephens as we were getting started was no surprise.

It began December 27, 1969, six months after Dar and I first saw the Hotel Golf. The very next day classes would begin with our first visiting teacher. Don Stephens and his bride were with us. Don and Deyon had gotten married shortly after our launchpad experience in the Bahamas. That night I asked Don if he would speak to the group. He stood before us now, his sturdy frame more filled out than it had been in the Bahamas, and told us how God had called him to missions. It was in a small chapel in the mountains, he related, and he was kneeling at the front when he first received the impression that he was to be in full-time work overseas.

A few weeks later, after hearing a teaching session on the power of a clean conscience, I noticed that Don was squirming in his seat. Finally he jumped to his feet.

"I have something to say. I exaggerated…no, I *lied* that first night we were here together when I told you guys how God called me. He did call me—the way I said…up to a point. But then I got carried away. I added some things that…weren't true. I lied. And I'm really sorry." Then he quickly sat down.

Soon Don's honesty was being matched all over the room as others unburdened themselves. It was an amazing time of honesty to watch as God's Spirit moved on people's hearts. Not every person, of course, chose to confess aloud that night, and that was all right, too. Each could have confessed quietly to God alone. That, in fact, is the only confession that brings salvation. But confession to man brings humility and unity and makes a repentant person ready to receive God's healing of mind, emotion, and body. Confession is good for the soul. We were also seeing the special advantages in confessing to a loyal and supportive group. I noticed as we told our faults to one another that we began to feel even closer, like a real family. At that moment, I could imagine myself being willing to die for Don, who had humbled himself. And for the others, too.*

Later, when the students went to their rooms, they wrote letters making relationships right with parents, pastors, teachers, and former sweethearts.

I remembered that little pile of letters on the desk in the Dawsons' basement room. And I remembered how, after that time of my own confession, the work of YWAM began to grow at a brand-new and accelerated pace.

Would the same thing happen to Don?

At the end of the summer of 1970, Dar, Karen, and I were walking in the forest by the hotel, talking about the school. I looked down at Dar, who was filling out with her second pregnancy, and thought that this day would tell us if our school idea really worked. Our thirty-six students had returned from their practical application trips all over Europe and as far away as Afghanistan, and soon we would hear their reports. As we strolled along through the pines, we looked forward to hearing the kids' stories—even though Dar and I had been able to personally visit a dozen of the locations in the previous weeks.

I wanted to hear about their times in the field, but I was even more eager to hear the students' future plans. Today was a big day because we would see the results of the guidance Darlene and I received together three and a half years ago, confirmed by Willard Cantelon, who had received exactly the same word. Guidance, like prophecy, has one tough criterion for validity: Does it work?

---

* Every individual has the right to confess his faults as the Holy Spirit convicts. (James 5:16, 1 John 1, and David's example in 2 Samuel 11–12). Two individuals have prayerfully volunteered their confessions in this book so that God's grace will be shown and others will be helped.

Would this group of young people yield new ministries under the umbrella of YWAM? Today we would know as the students gathered on the lawn outside the hotel.

Late that afternoon, with the Alps looking down on us, we were sitting in a circle of folding chairs in front of the hotel under the arbor of sycamore trees. Dar was struggling with two-year-old Karen, who was being drawn like a magnet to Deyon's two-month-old baby. Jimmy and Jannie were in the circle, just back from Afghanistan, where they had led a small team. I looked at Jim and Jannie and wondered how much longer before their prayers were answered for a baby of their own after six years of marriage.

As we sat in the lacy shade of the trees, the thirty-six young people began to tell about their adventures in Germany, Spain, France, Great Britain, Yugoslavia, Bulgaria, and Afghanistan. I filled everyone in on the people who weren't able to be with us at this time—by this point we had inched up to forty staffers worldwide, including Kalafi and Tapu and their team in New Guinea.

Finally it was the time I had been waiting for—the time to hear the plans of those around the circle. It wasn't a disappointment. Person after person believed that God was telling him or her to stay on with YWAM in autonomous yet related missionary work in specialized areas of need.

Was what I had longed and prayed for really happening? Yes, we really were starting the multiplication process I'd dreamed of for so long…young people coming to us for short-term service, some staying on for our school, then reaching out on their own to France, England, Germany, Spain. Jannie and Jimmy were going to Scandinavia.

I looked over at Don and Deyon Stephens sitting quietly at the edge of the circle, for they were the only ones who had as yet said nothing. Deyon's eyes were sparkling, her broad smile even wider. "Don?" I asked. "What's up?"

Don sat forward in his chair and told how he had been so afraid I'd call on him that morning, because until lunchtime he didn't know what he and Deyon were to do. They had been praying for weeks, but nothing seemed clear as to what they should do.

"I had about given up. Nothing seemed to light a fire, and we weren't getting any guidance. Then during lunch I picked up a new *Time* magazine from our bed. I opened it and started looking at the pictures of Munich, Germany, and the site they're building for the Summer Olympics two years from now in 1972. For some reason, I also remembered the thousands of Communist youth I saw marching in East Berlin not long ago, chanting slogans. It was eerie, because not one of those youths had any light in his eyes. They were like marching death."

He looked over to where I was sitting and drew a breath, hitting his chest with his palm. "Loren," he said, "I believe we're supposed to have Christians marching in Munich during those Olympics! I think it would be a great opportunity to meet all kinds of people from both sides of the Iron Curtain and tell them about Jesus Christ. Why, with all the athletes and visitors, it'll be like a world in miniature there!"

Something jumped inside me when he said it, and I knew it was right. And I wasn't the only one—exclamations of excitement and approval were buzzing around the circle.

Here was the idea of multiplication working at its best. YWAM was the catalyst for releasing people like Don. God had given this major idea to someone besides me in our little school. Remembering how Don had stood and humbled himself before the group, I was glad he was the one God had chosen. I trusted him.

"How many do you believe we should have there, Don?" I asked.

He dropped his eyes a moment and said, "Two hundred."

The number sounded low to me, but even that many young people sharing their faith in Jesus Christ would be quite a feat. Especially in the light of the housing shortages that I knew would accompany the Olympics.

So that was our winding-up session. I had a tremendous sense of excitement about the event. Later we had a time of group prayer, sending people off with blessings in a dozen separate directions to give themselves to the specific plans of ministry that the Lord had shown to them.

Finally Don and Deyon and their little one left, too. They piled their Ford minibus high with gear and left us to scout out Munich.

I had a feeling we were on the verge of something very big.

TWELVE

The Danger of Success

I WISH with all my heart that I'd known—early enough to prevent the pain—one most important principle of guidance: *The Lord will lead us into victory, but success itself is the most dangerous obstacle to properly hearing the voice of God.*

We had no hint of this principle as we moved into the intertwining adventures that lay just ahead.

It was a raw, cold day two years after Don Stephens first glimpsed the dream of taking volunteers to the Olympic Games. I was thinking about a giant Heidelberg press, worrying about where we were going to put it, as I hustled down a gray sidewalk in Copenhagen. The press weighed two tons, and we wanted to use it to print a million pieces of literature to distribute to the visitors who would be coming to the Munich Olympics just six months away. The press had been donated, along with money for paper and ink. Our only problem was that we had no place to put the huge press. It had to be delivered, set up, and producing in two weeks.

I stepped off the curb, dodged a Volvo, and hunched down into my overcoat, anxious to get back to the warmth of Jimmy and Jannie's small base-of-operations apartment.

Of course, a place to house a printing press was just a small part of the challenges that faced us. We had hundreds of young people coming to Munich. Don admitted that he'd hedged when he first guessed we might have two hundred volunteers. After recruiting in the United States, Canada, South Africa, and Europe, we now knew we would have closer to one thousand. And we still didn't have an adequate place to house that many workers!

Don had been to Munich several times looking for accommodations. On his first trip, nearly two years earlier, he had learned that every large facility within a two-hour drive of Munich had already been booked.

"We have to at least find a garage or something so we can get that press rolling!" had been the last decision as Don and I frantically searched for an answer to the immediate need.

I wasn't really worried about housing for the press or for the kids either. Having seen God provide countless times before, I knew something would turn up. It always did. I thought back over the past two years and how easily things had been happening. We had found the formula and it was working! "It's all there, for any Christian to discover," I reminded myself, perhaps a bit proudly. "Just get the word of the Lord on what He wants to do, declare His Word aloud, and then watch it happen."

A year earlier, about one month before the birth of our son, David, God had spoken to us to buy the Hotel Golf. Up to that point, all that YWAM had owned were a few typewriters, a small used printing press (quite a step up from the old mimeograph we had used in the days when Bob and Lorraine were helping with our first newsletters!), and a meager collection of used vans and cars. But God had said buy, so we declared it. I set my mind and spirit never to doubt that the necessary money would be there, and that it would arrive on time.

Every week a little more arrived for the purchase of the Hotel Golf. We all did our part, too. We were amazed at how God was working as we watched our young people giving sacrificially with us for the purchase. Dar and I believed God was saying we should sell our "nest egg" house in La Puente and give that money. So we did.

On the very last day the money was due, we were still lacking $10,000. I went by the post office to check our mail one last time before going to give our payment. There, waiting in our box, were donations from several people who believed in what we were doing here in Switzerland. I found it very hard to believe that the total was $10,060! Just out of curiosity, I watched the box for four days after we had paid the full amount, but nothing came in, not a dime.

I just knew that the housing in Munich would also work out. And we'd find a place to put the printing press. *But it had better be soon!* I thought, considering the Olympics were only six months away.

And sure enough, a few days later the phone rang. It was Don, and he was very excited. "Loren, I think we've found a place for the printing press—*and* a thousand kids!"

"Yeah? That's great, what is it? A warehouse? A camp?"

"Well, no...it's a castle."

As he said the word *castle*, I heard that inner click. It was preposterous, but as Don described the castle that was for sale, I knew it was for us. When Don hung up I prayed about whether we were to buy the castle. As I prayed I began to grasp a further vision—this facility was not just for the Olympics, but for a permanent German base. Every hour the quiet "yes" inside me grew bigger.

A few days later I joined Don Stephens in Munich, and together we went to look at the castle. We drove for an hour away from the city, across flat farmland toward the village of Hurlach, and turned down a country road. There it was, standing on the horizon like a giant. Our castle! It had twin towers with onion-shaped domes. Inching our way through the gates and around a circular drive, we pulled up to a massive, ornately carved door and got out to crane our necks at the six-story castle and adjoining lower buildings.

"It's huge!" I whispered to Don.

We rang the bell, and soon the *hausmeister* was leading us through the building. From dungeon to attic, everything was in mint condition. It had been built in the sixteenth century, and the present owner, a children's social services group, had recently modernized the buildings at a cost twice the asking price! The castle had enough rooms and bathroom facilities for three hundred people. But with various cavernous attics and two acres of grounds, I figured we could temporarily house many more hundreds.

"We said we needed a garage, and there it is," laughed Don. "It just came with a castle attached!" We walked briskly toward an adjacent building, which was a garage large enough for our Heidelberg press.

"And out back," I said, "we can put up a tent for a large training session."

We drove back to Munich with a German interpreter, walked into a meeting of the owners, and made a proposal, using the detailed terms that I felt God had given me. We agreed to make a down payment within the week. Then we agreed to make another payment by the end of August, which would fall during our Olympics effort.

We came out a few minutes later with the keys to a castle. It was all so easy. Within one week, the money for the deposit came in from European Christian friends. Our faith was riding high. A few days later, the Heidelberg press was delivered to our castle at Hurlach, and our printers began to turn out Gospel papers written in German, English, and French.

At first it seemed the idea could not be from God.

It happened not long after Don moved into the castle in March 1972, just four months before the games. I was off on one more swing around the rim of the Pacific, urging young people to join us for the three-week effort in Munich. As I moved from country to country, I really wasn't expecting what God did next, partly because it had nothing to do with the Olympic Games. God was preparing us for events that were still distant.

I was flying from Seoul to Hong Kong, and the stewardess had just removed my lunch tray. We were flying south above the Yellow Sea. I lifted the shade that covered the oblong porthole, and there in the misty distance lay a body of land that I knew must be Mainland China. We should be near Shanghai, I reckoned, somewhere in that distant haze.

Suddenly God's voice broke into my thoughts. *It's time for you to pursue the ship.*

I was astonished. "Is this You, God?" was my automatic question. Ever since Hurricane Cleo in the Bahamas years before, I'd realized that we were to have a dual nature to our mission—loving God and helping people who were in need. And a ship would be a perfect tool to carry out both ministries. But the thought overwhelmed me. I could imagine all that a ship would entail—finding a skilled crew, satisfying international shipping requirements, and raising the enormous amount of money to keep a mercy ship afloat and adequately provisioned.

"God, if You're saying now is the time to begin, please help me to be certain. Taking on something this big would cost us dearly."

I had no idea how high the price would be.

In New Zealand a few weeks later, I had just finished speaking to young people about the Olympic outreach for Munich. I enjoyed coming back to this lovely country with its green, sheep-dotted hills. Here I had learned so many of the ways of God. I had met Kalafi Moala, Jim and Joy Dawson, and others who meant so much to me. Now we had a fine core of leaders for YWAM New Zealand. I told these men about the experience in the Bahamas and the word that God had given me again in the airplane over Shanghai. Was God leading us toward buying a ship?

Six of us gathered to pray. "Lord, we need Your help. You know how hard it would be just to gather the right people…" someone was saying. Suddenly we heard a knock at the door. Mildly annoyed at the interruption, I went to see who it was. There stood a weathered man of about thirty.

"What is it, sir?" I asked, glancing over my shoulder at my friends who were waiting to continue with our praying.

The man must have seen that he was interrupting, for he blurted out: "Why would God call a man to missions when he's just not qualified?"

It was an odd question. But a nudge in my spirit told me to listen to him carefully. "Come in, won't you?" I opened the door wide. "What do you mean, unqualified?"

"I mean," the man said, stepping uneasily into the room, "all I know is the sea. I've been a chief engineer and a skipper, and yet I know God is calling me to missions! They never go together, do they?"

We were overwhelmed at the direct way the Lord was answering us. The seaman, it turned out, wanted work right away, which we couldn't supply. Nevertheless, his coming by while we were praying for guidance caused a flurry of excitement. The first order of business was the Olympic outreach in Munich, but now we knew that God was giving us marching orders for the future.

I headed home, eager to fill Dar in on what had happened and to catch up on all the preparations that were happening for Munich. I wouldn't have time to go by New Guinea to see Kalafi and Tapu and their two little girls. They had twenty-five staff members, but I reassured myself that Kalafi was probably doing a great job.

Dar and I and our children, ages four and eighteen months, turned off the highway from Munich and headed through the flat farmland toward the castle. In just one week, hundreds of young people would be coming from literally every continent to this village. The sleepy hamlet with its half-timbered cottages, its pristine white Catholic church, and handful of shops was in for a booming three weeks of activity.

Kids with backpacks were already walking through the village. "Do you realize, Dar," I said, turning our car toward the castle, "there are only a thousand residents in Hurlach? We'll double the population in just one week."

Dar laughed. "Yes, and do you realize, Loren Cunningham, that ten years ago you told me your life goal was to see a thousand young people in evangelism? Here they are!"

It was an interesting, but not satisfying, remark. We now had goals way past that original number of workers. God had given us confirmation of goals for twin ministries that were already in embryo. Fulfilling those would take even more workers.

I pulled up the circular drive and stopped in front of the massive carved front door. Don had been eagerly awaiting our arrival, for he bounded out to greet us, followed by Deyon with their two-year-old blond doll. "Come back behind the castle, you guys. We have a surprise for you!"

As we walked around the castle, I was amazed at what I saw. There, just barely squeezed into the space between the castle and the back fence, was a large, striped circus tent!

"Loren, I had almost given up finding one, since it seemed every big tent in Europe had been rented. But then a dance was canceled…and so now we have our meeting place," Don said.

THIRTEEN

Munich:
The World in Miniature

ALL that week the kids came pouring in. A thousand of them. They represented fifty-two nations and fifty denominations. Jimmy and Jannie arrived in a VW camper. Jim and Joy Dawson were there—Jim, ever the elegant one, and straight-talking Joy, who would be one of the Bible teachers for the training we would be giving to all those young people in our tent.

The plan for the three weeks was a simple one. Each day, five hundred young people, under Don Stephens's leadership, would go into Munich and witness and hand out literature on the streets while the other five hundred, under my leadership, would stay back at the castle and get replenished with lots of teaching, prayer, and Bible reading. Then the following day, the groups would trade places. The kids would get up at five in the morning, take sack lunches on the train to Munich, and not return until midnight. We hoped to have marches in the city and a mammoth music festival toward the end of the three-week outreach for the Olympics.

From the very first day of the campaign, however, we met the worst kind of resistance we could imagine—*indifference*.

We were like uninvited guests at someone's party. The atmosphere in Munich was like a carnival. It was a tough assignment as we attempted to interrupt festivities to talk to people about important spiritual concerns. Sports was the giant idol—it had the world bowing at its feet. Athletic competition was being promoted as the answer to peace and brotherhood. The German authorities, anxious to have a smooth-running Olympics to show the world, forbade the marches we had planned and put us outside Munich for our music festival.

So we had to improvise. We specialized in small teams, sending some onto school campuses while others went into parks where young Communists and spaced-out street people congregated. Other teams held impromptu rallies throughout the city and on the Olympic grounds. In the Athletes' Village, our kids talked to participants from behind the Iron Curtain. When we found people who wanted to learn more, we brought them to a large store we'd turned into a coffeehouse. There we talked to them about Jesus.

We were getting fair results, but the going was rough. We'd been at work for two weeks, and the greatest challenge in that atmosphere of fun and competition was still the shrug-of-shoulder indifference we saw in so many people. The people were here for the excitement of the games, and eternal values seemed to hold little interest for many of them.

All of this excitement changed when the idol of world-brotherhood-through-sports cracked and fell.

I was speaking in the big striped tent early Tuesday morning, September 5, when I noticed unrest near the back. Whispers were passing down the rows of seats, and faces were darkening with worry. Finally a denim-clad volunteer hustled up the dirt aisle and handed me a note.

I read it in disbelief. Arab terrorists had broken into the Athletes' Village, killing two Israeli contestants and taking nine hostages. I announced the news to the young people, and we began to pray immediately.

We suspended classes, broke into small groups, and asked God to somehow and in some way bring good out of this tragedy. We learned later that the five hundred YWAMers who were in the city with Don were also praying wherever they were. They knelt in silent circles yards away from the police-cordoned area where the terrorists held the athletes hostage. Other YWAMers knelt on the sidewalks of downtown Munich. They knelt at our coffeehouse. And we held our breath together with the rest of the world.

Swiftly, in an explosion of violence, the drama ended, and nine more Israelis, five Arabs, and one German were killed.

Overnight the carnival of the Olympics turned into a funeral witnessed by the whole world. People milled about in the streets lost in grief and unbelief at what had happened. Suddenly our young people were accepted, for we were in Munich as emissaries of hope. We wept with the weeping, assuring them that Jesus Christ held the answer to tragedies like this. And hearts were open: On the very day of the terrorist attack, a young Israeli YWAM girl led an Arab Muslim to faith in her Messiah.

Dar and I could no longer stay at the castle out in the country. We had to go into Munich with the rest of our young people. We stood with a group in the entertainment area of the Olympic grounds, singing and directing attention to God. One by one, people filled the amphitheater, quietly listening to us. As we finished, an attractive German woman of about twenty came up and asked, "You are a Jesus people?"

Dar and I answered at the same time. "Yes." A look of intense longing came over the young woman's face.

"I'm not a Jesus people. But I want to be." We took her to the coffeehouse and introduced her to Don, who was fluent in German. He found out she had been wandering through Europe, trying to find meaning to life. She found it that night, announcing with a sweep of her arm, "Now I know Jesus. I am a Jesus people, too!"

After the Israeli athletes' tragedy, city officials changed their minds about us. One police officer told Don, "You Christians are the only good that has happened here in the last three weeks." They now allowed us to march, even donating thousands of flowers from city gardens for us to give out as we walked through the heart of the city, a thousand strong, in sympathy for the slain athletes.

We printed ten thousand newspapers on our Heidelberg press out in the castle garage. The papers were grabbed out of our hands as we marched through the city. They featured a picture of an Arab YWAMer and a Jewish YWAMer standing arm in arm, proclaiming that the only answer for world brotherhood was Jesus Christ.

The three weeks at the Olympics were over, having ended in a tragic drama that Munich would never forget. Though our outreach was over for us, our time there had allowed us to participate in people's sorrow. Despite the tragedy that had left the world in horror, we sensed it also marked a new beginning for YWAM.

Through generous gifts we met the payment on the castle and knew that we now had a permanent anchor place in Germany. Just before the big striped tent came down, we had an unusual offering. We told our young people they could either put money into the basket or take from the basket, depending on their guidance and plans. Many of the volunteers needed airfare because they had chosen to go to one of our twenty centers throughout the world and continue working with YWAM. Others chose to go to one of the three schools that had sprung up after our Lausanne prototype. In almost every case there was an added expense: the long trans-Atlantic or trans-Pacific phone calls back home to discuss new plans with mothers and fathers, because we stressed keeping lines of communication open with parents and churches.

The end of the Olympics allowed me to shift my attention, too. The next place where I needed special guidance was the ship. Somehow I knew what the ship would be like: about five hundred feet long, able to sleep several hundred, a floating campus for a school, and a cargo hold large enough to carry plenty of materials to needy people. We'd have medical teams aboard and hundreds of young people carrying the Good News to off-load at the international ports the ship would dock in. We would paint the ship white—symbolizing the purity of God.

When the third individual told me about an interisland ferry named the Maori for sale in New Zealand, I began to take notice.

In April 1973, thirteen months after God told me to pursue the ship, I headed for New Zealand to take a look at the Maori. We had already found a captain and other qualified crew members. Even now they were in Lausanne, going through our school and preparing for the future ministry of the ship.

Flying into Wellington, my plane made its final approach low over the harbor. The hilly city, which was wrapped around a bay, looked much like San Francisco.

Then, below me, I saw her. The ship I saw moored at the dock could only be the *Maori*. She was just as friends had described her, a black ship about 450 feet long with white upper decks and an orange and blue funnel, sitting squarely confident at the foot of Wellington's hills. I thought with assurance, *I am looking down on our destiny!*

A representative from the Union Steamship Company and one of our directors from YWAM New Zealand were with me as I climbed the gangplank onto the *Maori*. It really was a fine vessel. It had three decks above, two decks below, which would sleep 920, and a large car deck that would accommodate 120 vehicles or tons of cargo. The ship even had a restaurant and lounge and a small infirmary. I knew without even a second thought that this was the ship we'd been waiting for. We drove away, leaving the *Maori* sitting proudly at her mooring.

I didn't have a hint, not one—as we got go-ahead signals from many directions—that I was stepping into the saddest mistake we can make in seeking to hear God's voice. It is a mistake, ironically, that comes late in an adventure in guidance, this time right when everything seemed to be going very well indeed.

FOURTEEN ⤸

The Man in the Shadows

I REALLY was not all that interested in money—Dar and I and five-year-old Karen and two-year-old David still lived in four rooms in an annex of the Hotel Golf in Lausanne. I was, however, very interested in the *guidance* aspect of money, and it seemed we were rapidly being led to purchase the *Maori*. Four months after seeing the ship myself, I sent Wally Wenge, my administrative assistant, to New Zealand to negotiate with the Union Steamship Company for the vessel. We agreed to put down a deposit of seventy-two thousand dollars by September 4, 1973. The rest would be due in thirty days.

Right away we were encouraged about the decision to purchase the ship. A businessman called me from England saying that God was telling him to do something for YWAM. The amount he sent was more than enough for our deposit. Wally Wenge phoned to say that stories were appearing in the New Zealand press about some young missionaries claiming God told them to buy the *Maori*. The ship had been in service for a long time in New Zealand, and she had become something of a landmark. People were interested in our story. Soon everyone in the country knew about our deal.

We felt confident. And given the success we'd had in the past, that confidence seemed justified. We made some added statements to the press stressing the fact that God not only speaks to His people but also provides. The papers loved it. One headline read, "Youth Say, 'God Will Give Us The Ship!'" We announced that the ship would be sailing from New Zealand to California in thirty days, when the balance of our payment was due. She would arrive there mid-October—two months from now. I was riding high on the excitement of it all. And why not? Every day, we saw some new release for the ship—either a volunteer or money or a special offer. One company promised free paint to redo the *Maori* all in white; the interior decorator of the *Queen Elizabeth II* volunteered his services free of charge; some farmers promised grains and meat to take to the needy. Most important, a businessman from Manila promised the remainder of the purchase price. All he needed to do was get his funds out of the Philippines.

Everything seemed to be falling into place, and the fulfillment of the vision of the ship was happening fast.

Simply administering these releases of provision kept me spinning. One day I began to feel the need to slow down. In fact I needed a week alone with God to fast and pray about all the developments.

In that week everything changed.

I was sitting quietly praying with my Bible open to Hebrews. Suddenly the words of chapter 12, verses 26 and 27, leaped off the page. "*Yet once more I will shake not only the earth, but also the heaven...that those things which cannot be shaken may remain*" (NASB, italics added).

A rock hit the bottom of my stomach. "Oh no! I hope that doesn't mean the ship!"

The next day, with no little anxiety, I called our California office. Jim Dawson had become the administrator after he and Joy had joined us as full-timers.

"What came in for the ship today?" I asked Jim.

"Not a thing, Loren."

Odd, I thought. "Has our Manila businessman gotten his money out of the Philippines yet?"

Jim reported that there was no news from the Philippines. That seemed very strange. We all thought that was going to be routine. I was puzzled. The words on that page of Hebrews had had such power in them! Maybe they *did* mean the ship!

For the rest of my week of prayer, I struggled with this apparent warning-guidance, but nothing became clear. Perhaps I'd learn more when I met with ninety-three of our YWAM leaders next week in Osaka, Japan. We had good experience hearing God when we were all together.

Two weeks before our deadline for paying the Union Steamship Company, I kissed Darlene good-bye and set out for Osaka via (as it turned out) an important stopover in Seoul, Korea.

On my way I thought about how crucial these yearly leadership gatherings had become. In the thirteen years since our beginning, we had grown into a family of two hundred individual missionaries from fifteen countries, working in separate bases with local funding and autonomy. We were linked in our friendship and in spirit by a common call and vision. With such decentralization, YWAM depended on meetings like this upcoming one in Osaka. Our close relationships to one another were the glue holding us together.

That unique closeness we all shared made my position all the more difficult if that word from God about "shakings" did concern the ship. I cringed at the thought of facing my friends (Don Stephens would be there and Jim and Joy Dawson; my sister Jannie and her husband, Jim; Kalafi and his wife,

Tapu...scores of others) and telling them the ship was in serious jeopardy.

As the air miles passed, I began to think perhaps the warning I'd received in Hebrews did not refer to our ship. Bit by bit my confidence returned. When I got to the stopover in Seoul, I phoned my assistant, Wally Wenge, in New Zealand. He was very positive. Our 110 volunteers and crew members from ten nations were hard at work cleaning the ship and polishing it from stem to stern. *Good!* I thought.

The mood of confidence was the reason, I am certain, for my being so shattered by the strange event that followed.

Early the next morning, I was lying on the floor atop my Asian pallet bed praying. In three days I would be flying to Osaka for the leadership conference. The deadline for the final payment for the ship was now only ten days away.

I gradually quieted my mind, focusing on Jesus, yielding to Him and worshiping Him, ready to listen to anything His Spirit wanted to say in my mind.

Suddenly I was looking at a mental picture. It was not unlike the picture of the waves I'd seen seventeen years earlier. Only this time, the vision was terrifying.

I saw myself standing before a crowd of YWAM leaders. I announced with exuberance, "We've got the ship! God has given us the money for the *Maori!*" The crowd cheered wildly, waving their arms and shouting. Then all of a sudden I saw a figure standing in the shadows to my left, unnoticed by any of us. I looked closer at his face and saw that he was grieving. Then it hit me—this was Jesus! We were ignoring Him! We were cheering a ship and forgetting Jesus!

I buried my face in the pallet bed, unable to wipe away the horrible sight. "Oh, God! Forgive me! I have gotten my eyes on the ship You're giving us and have taken them off

You! I…we…do not deserve to have it! We don't want to rob You of Your glory and give it to a hunk of metal."

I cried a long time, and I felt that God had heard and forgiven me. But I knew my attitude wasn't the only one that needed correcting. I had a somber message to give to the leaders on Monday in Osaka. We had to do some serious business with the Lord before we thought about anything else.

It was all I could do to force a smile as we deplaned at the Osaka airport. Kalafi Moala's work with YWAM was located here in Japan, and Kalafi and Tapu had come to meet me. Kalafi hadn't changed, except that his square frame was filling out some. "You're looking more like a royal Tongan," I said, trying not to let my grief show for now. Kalafi's wife was shorter than he was, pretty, with black, soft curly hair and a shy smile. They began to bustle me toward their van, warning me about the rustic hostel they had found for our meetings.

"It's not the Ritz," Kalafi said.

We chatted about their work as we drove. Was it my imagination, or did Kalafi seem less lighthearted than I remembered? Maybe it was the years…he had been a slender eighteen-year-old when I first met him in New Zealand six years ago. Kalafi answered my questions, telling me enthusiastically about their work with the university students. As I listened to what God was doing through him, I dismissed my first impressions.

Kalafi parked in front of the two-story Spartan hostel in Otsu City, outside of Osaka. All my YWAM friends rushed up to greet me as we entered the terrazzo-floored lobby. The mood of every man and woman was upbeat, and I quietly nursed my dark secret.

An efficient Japanese matron issued me hard plastic slippers, a towel, and sheets; then I climbed the stone steps to my room. I threw the sheets onto a bunk and lay down. I wasn't looking forward to our first meeting that afternoon.

On the second floor was a conference room with three semicircular rows of chairs waiting for us to start our meeting. We settled into our places. *There won't be much to distract us*, I thought, looking at the bare room.

I stood up, and every eye riveted on me. I knew they were all expecting to hear the latest good news about the ship. I spoke instead about the vision God had given me—of Jesus grieving in the shadows while we praised a hunk of metal.

It was a simple story, really. Yes, God had told us to get a ship, and repeatedly He had confirmed His guidance, using all the ways we had learned for hearing His voice. He used the Wise Men Principle; He used scriptures that He seemed to lift off the pages for us; He used provision of money and people; and that inner conviction—but we had failed in the *way* we had carried out His guidance. We had subtly turned from the Giver to the gift.

The reaction of everyone was immediate and almost unanimous…and it was the same as my own had been when I was alone on my Asian pallet bed back in Seoul. The conviction of the Holy Spirit was evident in the room as some fell to their knees or on their faces. Someone began to cry. Soon we were weeping in repentance—strong men and women—crying for how we had grieved Him.

For six days we came together, not to rejoice because we had a ship, but to confess times in our lives when we had failed to put God first or had robbed Him of His glory. The confessions continued day after day. During one of the times, Kalafi spoke up. He stood, his face grave, and mentioned briefly that he was having trouble in his marriage. *Kalafi and Tapu were in trouble?* I asked myself, surprised. Kalafi didn't elaborate, and somehow with the weight of all that was being unearthed, I didn't get around to taking him aside to see if I could help.

Every day we came into the bare, austere meeting room expecting the heavy feeling of guilt to lift. And every day we found new areas in our lives and attitudes that needed purifying. A painful awareness of God's awesome holiness coursed through the room. We began to sense great corporate shortcomings. The biggest failure on our part was pride. To our horror we saw that we'd begun to think that Youth With A Mission was God's "favorite tool": We were "the most spiritual" mission; we had learned "more about faith" than others; we had "a corner on releases." We saw down into the deceit of our own hearts, and it was disgusting. For the first time, I glimpsed something of what it will be like to stand before God on Judgment Day.

There was nothing to do but throw ourselves on His mercy. On the seventh day as we were singing softly, suddenly a special, deep quietness settled over us. Immediately we all knew that Jesus had walked into that bare conference room on the second floor of a hostel outside Osaka. And in an instant He sovereignly removed all the guilt. We were clean, forgiven.

After a time of rejoicing, I kept thinking He would give some direction concerning the ship. But it didn't happen. I did not know what to do. I only hoped that our repentance had been in time and that somehow, with right priorities and our focus now on Him instead of on a tool, He would heal this situation and still give us the ship.

But no such healing came to us. The deadline for closing on the *Maori* arrived. I called Wally in New Zealand and told him what had been happening. He was, of course, as stunned as we were. I asked him to see if he could get an extension from the Union Steamship Company. Wally called back to say we'd been granted four weeks. But the crew, he said, had to move off the ship and stop the renovations. About half were going home, but sixty were staying and were being housed by Christians in Wellington.

"What about a loan, Loren?" Wally ventured. "Three people have offered to lend us money to buy the ship." But his voice lacked conviction. We both knew that accepting a loan at this time wouldn't be right.

We left Osaka limping, saying our good-byes, and went back to our individual duty posts around the world. I headed back to Dar, who had flown to California from Switzerland and was waiting, as numbed as we were from the new developments. She and I had fully expected to be in California to celebrate the *Maori*'s arrival.

Now, back in the States, Darlene and I settled down to some long prayer times. *Is this really You, Lord?* I found myself saying over and over again. Why had God not healed our ship ministry? Perhaps He would still do so in the three weeks before the new deadline on November 2. "Help us, dear Lord. Help us to understand what You're doing," Darlene prayed.

That prayer, at least, was answered. The insight came through one of the people who had been at the Osaka conference—Joy Dawson, who telephoned a few days later.

"Loren," Joy said, "I have just finished reading the story of Lazarus. I was reading the part where Jesus chose not to *heal* Lazarus. He waited instead until His friend died, then *resurrected* him. In this case, a resurrection brought more glory to God than a healing."

As I listened to her share what the Lord had shown her, my chest tightened.

"Loren, I believe God is saying this to YWAM right now—that He is giving us a choice. We can have a healing of the ship. But greater glory will come to Him if we accept a resurrection. The hard part is that if we let the ship die, something of us will die right along with it...our *reputation*. As for me and my little part in YWAM, I'd prefer the latter."

The certainty that Joy was speaking truth blocked out everything else. I knew the choice that was before me now. After we hung up, I prayed by myself to make sure, but the truth of what Joy had said only grew larger in my mind. God was giving us a chance to give greater honor to Him by letting our dream die so that He could resurrect it.

First, of course, plans for the *Maori* did have to die. Really die. And we had to "die" right along with them. Remembering all that had been written about us in the New Zealand papers, especially those times when we said flatly that God would give us a ship, I knew I had to make something right with the people in New Zealand. People's trust in God may have been hurt, and they would easily doubt that He speaks and provides.

Though it was a difficult and humbling experience, I sat down and wrote a letter to a New Zealand newspaper. The letter was printed, telling how God had guided us to buy a ship but we had failed by giving greater honor to the ship than to the Lord. The response was immediate and hostile, especially among some Christians who saw us as having made presumptuous claims.

What could I say? All I knew was that ever since the day four weeks before when I had read in Hebrews that God was going to shake what could be shaken, not one dollar had come in for the ship (in total contrast to the prior six months), not one item pledged, not one additional worker or service released. Nothing. And still the Philippine government refused to budge regarding our friend's personal funds that he had pledged. This abrupt standstill had all happened, even though there was no way for people to have known of any change. Suddenly the flow had been turned off, and only God could have done it.

The gracious gentlemen of the Union Steamship Company again gave us an extension—one week this time. We accepted, because we had no idea what shape God's resurrection would take. But the end seemed near. It was like watching a loved one wasting away with a terrible disease.

To make matters even worse, we still had ninety students coming to our team houses in L.A., ready to join the ship for an on-board school. I made the necessary calls and gave them the choice of meeting us for a school in Hawaii instead.

I must confess that my heart was very heavy when I flew out of Los Angeles International Airport a few weeks later with my family, heading for Hawaii. Then, as we drove over Pali Highway from the Honolulu airport, I reflected on how different our visit was this time. The sunshine was the same, and the brilliant blue water surrounding Diamond Head was the same. Nothing was different about the plumeria trees with their yellow, white, and pink flowers. No, the difference was inside. The times I had come to Hawaii before had been joyful expectation—trying a brand-new experiment, rejoining Darlene after a long absence, planning a school that was different from anything we had ever seen.

This time we were coming to Hawaii to wait.

We pulled off the highway into a camp in Kaneohe on the other side of the island from Honolulu. Some of our YWAM workers in Honolulu had located this camp, which was suitable for housing our staff and students for a while. Beside the parking lot, facing Kaneohe Bay, were the dining room/meeting hall and kitchen. On the parking lot was a pay phone—not a booth, just a plastic bubble on a pole protecting the phone. It was the only phone available in the camp. I knew I'd be spending a lot of time in front of that bubble as we groped our way through the morass of the *Maori*.

Darlene and I and the children made our way to the cab-
ins, wooden structures with walls only two-thirds of the way
up the sides and topped with screens. There were no closets
and no plumbing; the bathrooms were in separate buildings.
It was just a camp.

But it was in this rustic setting that we received the most
startling of guidance experiences we had ever had up to that
time.

FIFTEEN

Three Steps to Hearing God

WE EXPERIENCED no hint of guidance in the early stages of this next unfolding of God's plan for our lives. It seemed we were only waiting. The ship was dead. Our reputations had been seriously bruised. But what made Dar and me most uncomfortable was the lack of clear direction.

"But are we being obedient, Loren?" Dar asked as I groused around, unpacking. Well, yes. I did think we were being obedient. "Then let's just listen. God will show us what He's doing!"

Dar busied herself making a home out of our tiny cabin at Kaneohe. The place barely had enough room for two sets of bunks. Dar strung up a clothesline, marking out a closet, put my briefcase on the floor, and announced that it was my office. And, of course, Dar brought out Karen's and David's own bowls and cups and their pictures of grandparents, aunts, uncles, and cousins. It wasn't too different from the tent-house, with boxes for furniture, that my folks had lived in during their pioneering days years before in Somerton, Arizona.

Virtually all of the ninety-two students showed up! I was astonished at the wonderful flexibility of youth. Jim and Jan Rogers came out, too. When we all gathered in the camp dining room and I explained what was happening, everyone joined in, praying for guidance and waiting expectantly. In the next few days, I spent lots of time at the bubble-topped phone in the parking lot talking to Wally Wenge in New Zealand about the *Maori*. The Union Steamship Company was extending the deadline one day at a time now.

The November winds and rains started, blowing in through our screen-topped bungalows. Soon we were locked in a mire of mud at our camp. When I asked God if we were doing what He wanted us to do, He just said, "Yes, the waiting won't last forever." More days passed, and I could still see no direction.

The breakthrough started one amazing night. I had decided to stay up all night and pray, asking three of the school staff, Jimmy and Jannie and Reona Peterson, to join me. Dar felt she was to stay with the children. The four of us walked to a small wooden annex at about 10:00 P.M., turned on the light, and went in. We knelt down on the rough floor beside some folding chairs. We followed the Three Steps to Hearing God that I had first learned from Joy Dawson in New Zealand. First, we took Christ's authority to silence the enemy. Second, we asked the Lord to clear from our minds any presumptions and preconceived ideas. Third, we waited...believing He would speak in the way and in the time that He chose.

A cool breeze stirred in from the bay, and gecko lizards chirped on the walls as we waited for God to speak in our minds.

We had a spirited time of praying for the ship ministry, then we waited again. The pointed black hands on the big wall clock read 11:00 P.M. Reona said a scripture reference had come into her mind: Luke 4:4. I remembered the time I'd initially observed this kind of guidance on my first visit to New Zealand. People would "hear" a scripture reference in their minds without knowing what the verse said. The key, we were taught there, was complete yieldedness to Jesus. We weren't playing some kind of game, pulling a reference out of the air. We were waiting, listening, and focusing our minds on Jesus alone to hear His voice on the matter. Then if He told us to look up a particular verse, we did so, knowing that God could use whatever means He chose to guide His people. Now, in that all-night prayer session, when we looked up the reference Reona had heard, we found a verse encouraging us to continue listening for God's voice—the passage in Luke where Jesus said that man lives by every word that comes from God.

Again we returned to silence. The hands of the clock swept to 1:30 A.M., but an air of anticipation kept me alert. I knew God was about to speak.

Another long time of silent seeking followed. It was surprising to see that the clock said 3:30. And I saw that my poor sister had fallen asleep, kneeling at her chair. Then suddenly the three of us quickly began to get words from God. Two impressions came into my mind very strongly. One was the word *Kona*. I knew that was a place on the Big Island, though I'd never been there. The second was a mental picture of a lighthouse on the Big Island, with rays beaming across the Pacific toward Asia.

I didn't understand what God was trying to say to us. The question on my mind was a resurrected ship ministry. Yet God was saying Kona and a lighthouse. I broke the silence and told Reona and Jimmy the impression I'd had (Jannie was still asleep), then suggested we go back to God for

"Round Two." "Lord," I prayed, "help us understand what You are saying."

As we continued in prayer, more thoughts came to us. The idea surfaced of some kind of school that was not another of our regular Schools of Evangelism but one that would be much broader in its training. Reona heard God speak about a farm, of all things. And the biggest puzzle of all: A picture came of a big white ship in a bay.

The black hands on the clock now read 5:30 in the morning. My mind was reeling with all this brand-new information. A lighthouse. A large school. The Big Island. Kona. A farm. A white ship in a bay. How was this to all fit together?

Jimmy woke Jannie, and we stood up stiffly. I thanked the others for joining me and went down the dark, muddy path to our cabin. I crawled into my bunk and sank into sleep, exhausted yet exhilarated.

It seemed only minutes until Dar was shaking my shoulder gently, telling me it was time to wake up. I quickly told her about the incredible night, then hurried to the dining room for the morning school session. The students were already sitting at the long tables that had been wiped clean from breakfast. Ninety-two faces looked up at me. Most were young people—girls with long straight hair parted in the middle, wearing jeans or granny skirts. The fellows were uniformly in jeans, some with long hair and beards, others cleanshaven.

"A few of us just spent a very interesting night hearing from the Lord," I began. "But I don't know if God wants me to tell you what He said. So we'll wait to see if He says any of the same things to you." I ran through the same steps for listening to the Lord that we had used: take authority over the enemy, clear away your own preconceived ideas, then listen for Jesus' voice.

Then we waited in silence.

"Who wants to be first?" I asked after many minutes.

Shyly, a moon-faced girl with round, rimless glasses spoke. "This sounds funny, but I just get this impression of a big letter *K*."

Strange, I thought. "Anyone else?"

A guy with a blond beard quickly spoke. "I got the word *Kona!*" Now I was getting excited. Someone else got *volcano.* The only active volcanoes in Hawaii were on the Big Island.

The incredible morning went on, and the kids continued to pop up with words from God all over the room. "I see a picture of a big place—I think it's some kind of school," one boy said. Someone else mentioned a farm, and someone saw a white house on a hill.

My pulse was pounding with excitement. So much was being repeated from last night that, frankly, I had trouble *believing* what I heard. I was glad ninety-two people were there who could be witnesses to the amazing way God was confirming what I'd heard during our all-night prayer vigil.

The part that really stirred me came right at the end of the seeking session. One girl saw a ship. She said it was white, and it lay at anchor in the bay of an island.

What on earth had been happening? Two weeks passed after that unbelievable all-night seeking experience. We had had an amazing glimpse into the future. But now I had to come to grips with present realities...the death of a ship and sixty crew members who I knew had been deeply wounded. So in early December I went to New Zealand. Wally Wenge met me at the Wellington airport. His face was gray.

"There's no point waiting to tell you, good friend. It's official—the Union Steamship Company has just closed the negotiations. We've lost our ship."

Neither of us said much as Wally drove me to the harbor to see our deceased dream. December was early summer in the

Southern Hemisphere, and the sun sparkled on the bay, a scene that did not match our somber moods. Wally and I stood in front of the *Maori*, which was tied to the dock with its gangplank up, forbidding entrance. I suddenly realized that we were both silent, as if we were standing before a casket.

Then we went to see the sixty remnant crew members. I told them about Lazarus. "If we're right in our guidance, the *Maori* is not going to be 'healed' for us. She is now dead, and the Lord will resurrect the dream in whatever fashion He chooses."

Looking out over the faces of the men, women, and teenagers who had given so much, I could feel the hurt they were experiencing. Some had come to New Zealand from far away for the dream. Many had given up good positions, sacrificing salaries and promotions. Together they had spent thousands of hours cleaning and scrubbing the *Maori*, putting love into the sudsy water on her decks. Losing the ship hurt them the most.

When I got back to Hawaii, I knew of someone who had to be told about the end of our dream. It was raining again, and I huddled under an umbrella as I stood at my pay phone in the parking lot of the Kaneohe camp. I gave the operator the number I wanted: the residence of the man in England who had given us the money for the ship deposit. The large deposit we had just forfeited. Miserably I hunched under my umbrella as the phone rang on the other end of the line. I felt a little like I'd felt when I was ten and had lost Mom's five-dollar grocery money.

The clipped British voice answered, and I plunged right in. I explained what had happened, including the picture of a grieving Jesus and the confessions of our sins, especially our pride, in Osaka. I explained how our confession opened the door to God's guidance again and that He had given us a choice. We could either "heal" this situation with the Maori or take a harder road and trust Him for a resurrection of our dream in whatever manner He chose.

"What you're trying to say, Loren, is that you've lost the deposit money," my friend said.

"That's...that's right."

The only sound coming over my bubble-topped phone at Kaneohe was the crackle of the cable connection. Finally my British friend spoke. "I consider my money well invested, Loren! God has used it to get your organization humbled before Him. I expect you to move ahead with a special power now. Congratulations!"

Now I was really humbled. What a man of God this English businessman was!

It was dawn in Kaneohe, Hawaii, but I was already awake. A month had passed since we had lost the ship. Dar, Karen, David, and I lay on our bunks in our screened cabin. Our suitcases were packed, waiting by the door. We were going home to Switzerland.

Lying there in the dawn light, I thought back over the past ten weeks of school. Those weeks of training with all those young people were to have been on our ship. Instead we held classes in a muddy camp. I was amazed at how well those kids adapted—not just to the physical miseries, but to the uncertainties. And now it was time to go home to Switzerland.

As I thought about our home, it was a little perplexing. I had an inner intuition that told me I'd be back here in Hawaii someday. Despite all the wind, rain, and mud, I had felt roots going down. Especially since that amazing all-night seeking session, followed in the morning by the kids having the same strange guidance—which so far, at least, nobody fully understood.

Our plane settled into the wintry valley by Lake Geneva. Don Stephens met us, his straight brown hair all but covered with a Russian-style fur hat. Don drove us home to the Lausanne hotel. The familiar square building looked welcoming by its evergreen forest. The hotel was now painted beige, and the old peeling green shutters were freshly done in chocolate brown.

We stood for a moment in the parking lot, our breath hanging in clouds, and recalled how we had first seen this building all boarded up more than four years earlier. We'd moved in with dreams and little else and begun to clean out the cobwebs. Since then almost all of those dreams had come true. We'd sent out thousands of workers to sixty countries, acquiring bases of operation in thirty-five locations.

Just one very important dream had not come true. *The ship*.

Don was dragging our suitcases out of his car, so I hurried to join him. When we reached our apartment in the hotel annex, David, age three, plumped his teddy bear on his bed across from his five-year-old sister's, and finally we were home.

Except somehow I didn't feel like it.

Could that very reaction be a part of what God was saying to us? Over the next weeks as we settled into the familiar routine, I had trouble focusing my mind. One morning during a class I tried to analyze my discontent. Don had done a great job in my absence. Reports came in from all over Europe about the creative, innovative evangelism of the kids under his leadership.

Don was now talking to the kids in the classroom about outreach plans for the summer. Suddenly I saw him look toward me uncertainly. I could almost read his mind. Perhaps he should be checking with me first? The moment passed and

Don went on talking, but not before I realized the multiplication principle had really taken place. Don was the leader at this base now, and the time had come for me to move on to new adventures of my own.

It was a strange time for someone interested in guidance. Although I was clearly being led *away* from one area, I was not as clearly being led to another. I wasn't supposed to stay in Europe; that seemed certain. And the ship was gone. We had lost her irretrievably.

One day while I was sitting in my favorite chair, a rocker, in our annex apartment, Wally Wenge called from New Zealand.

"Loren, I thought you'd want to know that the *Maori* was towed out to sea today. She's been sold for scrap to a Taiwan salvage company. Some of our crew stood on the dock and watched the tug pull her away...."

I hung up and looked out on the fog-shrouded mountains, feeling the same helplessness I had felt when Aunt Sandra and, later, Aunt Arnette had died of cancer. The happy chatter of Karen and David drifted in from their room. When Dar came in a few moments later with mugs of steaming cocoa, I told her about Wally's phone call.

"The *Maori* is dead...dead, Darlene." She didn't say anything. We just sat there, looking out the window at the January mist. I thought about the pain that had followed in the four months since God had said He was going to shake what could be shaken. "I've never felt so...without direction."

"I know, sweetheart. We've lost our axhead."

I knew immediately what guidance principle Darlene was referring to. Duncan Campbell, who had taught for three years at our schools, had told us about Elisha and his school of the prophets. One of Elisha's students lost the head off his ax. Elisha instructed the young man to go back to the place where he last knew he had it. There, at that spot, God gave the young man the tool he needed. Sometimes, Duncan said, we momentarily lose our axheads—our best cutting-edge tool for ministry, which is the clear voice of God. It helps to go back to the place where we last knew we had heard the sharp edge of God's voice.

Where was the last place that we knew God was speaking to us?

I saw it very clearly.

"There's no doubt where that was, Dar," I said. "The last place we had our axhead was at that all-night prayer meeting in Hawaii." And what had He said? We had gone into that night asking God about the *Maori*, but instead He talked to us about a lighthouse for the Pacific and Asia on the Big Island.

Dar and I talked late into the afternoon—our cocoa growing cold and forgotten on the table beside us—as we recalled the words God had given so mysteriously to separate groups. God had spoken about the Kona Coast of the Big Island, about a big white house on a hill, about a farm, a new kind of school…even about a white ship in a bay. Surely that was where the axhead lay.

We found ourselves particularly intrigued by the idea of the lighthouse for the Pacific and Asia. For some time, we had grown increasingly aware of the great needs of that area, for it was the least evangelized region in the entire world. Sixty percent of the earth's population lived there, yet only one percent of Asians claimed a personal relationship with Christ.

We *both* now knew the direction of our next adventure. We'd be expanding our horizon. Hawaii, after all, was a steppingstone to Asia.

"We'll move to the Big Island permanently!" I said.

Dar laughed when I said the word *permanently*. I knew she was thinking of our nine years together, spent in tents, schoolrooms, and camps. Why, our kids' home was almost literally a suitcase with pictures of their family attached to the inside lid. I laughed with her, suddenly relieved that we again clearly saw the path that lay ahead for our family.

It was just as well that neither of us knew just how hard it would be to claim that spot of ground for our steppingstone into Asia.

SIXTEEN

Kalafi Comes Home

SOMETHING was happening! I could feel it in the air. It was three years after Darlene and the children and I said good-bye to our home in Lausanne. Dar had left her favorite wildflowers in the fields around the Lausanne hotel and was substituting for them the brilliant flowers of Hawaii's Big Island.

I turned the YWAM van onto the access road leading to the tumbling-down buildings, half-hidden by a jungle of bushes and weeds. The sign on the main road, with some letters missing, read "Pacific Empress Hotel." Darlene and I and Karen and David, eight and six now, sat squeezed together in the front seat. Ten more YWAMers were crowded into the back of the van. Three other vehicles followed close behind. We were all dressed in our oldest clothes for the dirty job ahead. When we got to the potholed parking lot, Karen summed it up well.

"What a mess!"

And yet, I am sure we were all seeing the property with other eyes, too. The Lord was at work. I looked at the tangle

of tropical vines that half obscured the quadrangle of buildings. Eight years ago, before declaring bankruptcy, it had
been the Pacific Empress Hotel. The gently sloping forty-five
acres surrounding the property had once been the hotel's golf
course. We had secured all this land, in its prime location,
with just a little money down.

"At least we have a beautiful view," offered Dar. She was
certainly right! Above us rose the peak of Hualalei, the
extinct volcano, which gave us abundantly rich land. Below
us stretched out a panoramic view of Kona Bay with its glit-
tering, turquoise water. As I looked out across the bay, I could
imagine a large white ship anchored there.

We went to work clearing the overgrowth. Hefting a machete
and hoe, I plunged into what had once been a landscaped
tropical garden around the swimming pool. All over the
property, volunteers from among the hundred staff and students at our present School of Evangelism were attacking the
mess.

As I fell into the rhythm of hoeing, kneeling, and pulling
the fist-thick weeds, I began to think about the quite remark-
able results of that all-night seeking session in the Kaneohe
camp four years ago.

With one puzzling exception, everything God had shown
us in Kaneohe had come to pass. We were, indeed, on the Big
Island. More pointedly, we were on the Kona Coast of the
Big Island, just as the fellow with the blond beard had pre-
dicted. And, as foreseen that night, we now owned a fifty-
five-acre farm. A man had walked up to me and said God had
told him to give it to us. And the large white house on the
hill that we had seen? That was a mansion a few miles away
that was now YWAM property, too, housing staff and students
for our new Discipleship Training Schools.

It seemed on the surface that we were fulfilling the mandate God had given us. Why, then, were Darlene and I still restless? *It just didn't make sense,* I said to myself as I pulled up another fistful of weeds growing in the lava. Yet over the past three years here on the Big Island, both of us had felt God had something more for us. One day, about a year before, I found out why when a question formed in my mind: *Loren, have you checked your life lately against your original call?*

It was a principle of guidance that I had been neglecting. Regularly we ought to check our progress against our original mandates. My calling was clear: to preach the twin character of the Gospel. Through Jesus Christ it is possible to love God with all our hearts and to love our neighbors as ourselves.

How successful—I'd asked myself during that review time—*had we been in taking that twin love to all the world?*

We'd not done too good a job, I felt, reaching our neighbor at the point where he was hurting. Ever since my time in the Bahamas after Hurricane Cleo, I'd dreamed of a ship that would go on mercy missions, helping us love our neighbors in their needs. Our first effort had been put on the altar because it robbed Jesus of His glory. But even in that disappointing loss, we'd had encouragements to hold on to our dream. One in particular meant a lot to me: Somewhere in our packed boxes, waiting for a wall to hang it on, was a plaque my mother had sent me. It said, "Don't Give Up the Ship."

And what of the identical twin—learning to love God with all our hearts and minds and strength? We had been hard at work in this area. The Good News had often been communicated by Christians in "religious" settings—usually large meetings in a church somewhere. But the secular world was using so many other ways to communicate its messages: the arts, entertainment, family, education, media, business, and government.

That day as I was touching base with my original calling, the vision of what God wanted me to do expanded.

Suppose—my heart raced—suppose we trained young people, especially Asians and Pacific Islanders, in these very same strategic areas of communication? Our purpose would be to release thousands of young people into these mind-molding streams of society as a multiplication factor for missions. In our training we'd stress relationships as much as head knowledge—relationships with God and with one another. We would use a floating faculty of experts who would come alternately to live with the students in the village lifestyle of Asia and the Pacific. The emphasis would be on learning through doing.

And now here we were, standing on the grounds of our university.

"You do have a sense of humor, Lord!" I said above the swish-chop noise of my machete as I hacked through a bougainvillea vine. "Only You could be creative enough to take this old hotel and turn it into a university." I thought of the way Harvard, Yale, and Princeton had started as equally struggling dreams of men who wished to focus on the Gospel. It seemed an ongoing process. Now U of N, the University of the Nations, would follow in the grand tradition in one respect at least—we were starting with nothing but a conviction and a Lord who guides.

Yet for now we were beginning the horrendous challenge of clearing land and repairing the buildings of the old hotel. David ran up to me with the exuberant excitement of a six-year-old about a tractor that had just arrived.

"Come look, Daddy! The tractor is pulling up the prickly bushes with a chain. Come look!"

Gratefully, I put down my machete and took David's hand and walked with him toward the welcome tractor. In that brief moment I saw into the future. I saw the day when thousands of young men and women would walk over these same grounds and out into the world as missionaries, communicators of God's grace.

If the grounds were a problem, the buildings were worse. Dar and I and the children walked through the dilapidated quadrangle of the old hotel.

"Do you realize there are ninety-nine rooms here and one hundred toilets?" I said to Darlene.

"And all of them," Dar said with a shudder, "are a mess!"

Our family had a special goal for that afternoon. We needed to find some rooms in the complex to serve as our home. Frankly, nothing seemed attractive. Every one of the four buildings was in acute disrepair. Much of the wood was termite-ridden, and some rooms reeked of urine from the squatters who had occupied the hotel until we bought it. Rats and cockroaches came and went as they pleased.

"I told you you'd be living very simply if you married me, Dar. But this?" I said, sweeping my arm to indicate a pile of rotting debris. "I don't see how even you can make the children feel at home here." I spoke laughingly, tousling Karen's hair, but I really wondered how Dar would manage. We had been married fourteen years, and we didn't even have a car or furniture of our own. Since coming to the Hawaiian islands, Dar and I and the children had moved eighteen times. Eighteen moves in three years!

"Don't worry, Loren," Dar said. "It'll look totally different when it's cleaned up!"

Dar finally chose three third-floor hotel rooms for us. The rooms had adjoining doors and a carpet that had once been blue. When we walked into the bathroom, I thought the fixtures had never been cleaned!

But how eager our YWAMers were to help. Over the next two weeks, scores of young people pitched in. The girls cleaned the toilets—all one hundred of them. The boys specialized in shampooing the filthy carpets. We had shifts of young men working all day and all night, going from room to room with a shampooer we'd rented from Pay 'n' Save.

At last Darlene and I and the children moved up the hill from our last quarters downtown in the village of Kailua Kona. We plopped our suitcases down on the now brightly cleaned blue carpet and looked out through the picture window over the coconut palm trees toward the gleaming bay. Dar was already getting out the children's cups, bowls, and pictures. "Here we are kids," she said, handing Karen and David their precious ongoing symbols. "Let's make ourselves a home."

A few days after moving in, I sat on a borrowed folding canvas chair on our porch—or *lanai*, as we call it in Hawaii—talking with a professor named Dr. Howard Malmstadt.

One of the principles we use in seeking guidance is *ongoing confirmation*, similar to the road signs you would look for on an unfamiliar highway. It was while we were sitting there on those folding canvas chairs that I saw just such a sign. Howard Malmstadt was a leading scientist and professor at the University of Illinois in Urbana when I first met him.

Now, as we sat on the lanai, I told Howard that God had been leading us to start a university. It would be a very special kind of spawning place—a place that would teach young people how to know God intimately and then make Him known in the influential areas of society.

"I know," he said quietly. "God already told me."

Howard went on to explain that he had recently been asked to allow his name to be considered for the presidency of a Midwestern university. When he prayed about the offer, a startling thought dropped into his mind: He was to go to Hawaii instead. "Why Hawaii?" "Because, I am going to give a university to YWAM," God answered. "It will be in Hawaii, and you will be a part of it."

As encouraging as these clear directions were, other areas gave far less comfort. The most wrenching of these was in the life of our dear Kalafi. For two years, Kalafi had fallen into the worst troubles imaginable.

I'd heard the first warning bell about Kalafi four years earlier, in 1973, at the Osaka conference when he spoke of problems in his marriage with Tapu. Dar and I met with them at our next conference a year later. We found a quiet room, closed the door, and listened as they told their sad story. The "marital problem," we learned, had been a girl.

"I kissed her, Loren," Kalafi said. "It never went any further than that! I confessed it to Tapu and to the other leaders under me. I thought it was over."

But Tapu had been deeply wounded. She couldn't forget the betrayal. There was more—details Dar and I didn't want to hear. We prayed with both of them, and they cried and spoke words of contrition. At first we thought their troubles were over and done with, but something wasn't right. I couldn't define it myself, but I knew their marriage still had a weakness. I tried to get Kalafi and Tapu to stay on with us in Hawaii, to be part of the next school, but Kalafi refused.

"No," he said, "we've been offered a free house in California. I think we should drop out of ministry for a while. We want to get our marriage together again...." It didn't sound altogether right to me somehow, but I didn't insist.

Within weeks of their arriving in California, our worst fears came true. Word came from the parents of a girl Kalafi had started seeing on the mainland. They were afraid their daughter and Kalafi were having an affair. Tapu, I learned, was also seeing someone else. I flew to Los Angeles to talk to Kalafi. Although I gave him every chance to speak honestly about what was happening in his life, he chose not to do so. From his lighthearted banter, I almost believed I had heard unfounded rumors.

When I got back to the Big Island, however, I received another call from the parents of the girl. I knew now that I had to confront my friend. I reached him at home. "Kalafi," I said, my voice echoing over the trans-Pacific line, "you must realize the seriousness of what you're doing! Come back now. It's still not too late."

His response was an awful silence.

The next week I got a letter. I tore it open and read, "I respect God, Loren, but I can't be a hypocrite. I need to live my own life. Please don't try to contact me again for a while."

Tears stung my eyes, but I wasn't giving up. I remembered another time when persistence had mended a broken relationship—when I kept calling my aunt Arnette in Miami until at last she agreed to see me.

A few months after Kalafi's letter, I saw Joy Dawson again, and we picked up our intercessory prayer for Kalafi. "God, give him another chance!" we begged, unashamed of the tears running down our cheeks.

We found out later that at the very time we were interceding for Kalafi, he was in a bar with several other young men. He had quickly plunged into sin, becoming the first each night to start drinking and the last to remain standing in the fights that often broke out. He had even started carrying a gun. On this night, he was in his favorite bar doing his best to get fighting drunk when a slip of a girl scooted into the booth beside him. Above the raucous music, the girl began to tell Kalafi how she had once gone forward in a Billy Graham meeting. Kalafi looked at her in surprise: None of his new friends knew his background. The girl told Kalafi she wished she had stuck with that decision.

"Kalafi, I'm so afraid," she finished. "I know I'm going to die and go to hell!"

At this Kalafi roared, shouting above the din of the barroom the astonishing words, "*God, get off my back!*"

Darlene and I were again in Los Angeles. We decided to go to Kalafi's house on the off chance that we'd find him at home. Our timing was amazing. We arrived just as Kalafi came to collect his belongings; he was moving out for good. I saw a hardness I had never known existed. When we asked about Tapu, Kalafi kept on packing. All he knew was that Tapu was singing in a nightclub in Inglewood. He didn't know where she was living, but he thought it might be an apartment on one of the north-south boulevards.

Dar and I drove to Inglewood feeling stupid. How could we ever find anyone in this maze of city streets, crowded with apartments? "God, You know where Tapu is," I prayed. "Would You please lead us to her?"

How can I describe what happened next? It took me a long time even to believe it myself. We were driving east along Imperial Boulevard, praying that God would show us which street to turn on. I crossed Inglewood Avenue and came to Hawthorne Boulevard and felt I should turn back to Inglewood Avenue. "Yes," Dar said, "that's right." I turned south onto Inglewood Avenue and drove slowly for four blocks. Then the Holy Spirit's voice spoke into my mind. *Stop here.*

"Let's try that one," I said, and Dar agreed right away. The apartment was a fading, green stucco, two-story building—almost identical to a dozen on both sides of the boulevard.

As we got out, we had to step over broken toys and bicycles on the sidewalk. We found a little girl who said a woman matching the description we had given lived in an apartment on the second floor. We walked up the stairs and knocked.

Tapu opened the door, clutching her bathrobe. Her eyes widened, and she backed into her living room. "How ever did you find me? Come in, but I can't talk! I have to go!"

We pleaded with Tapu, but it was useless. After a five-minute visit, standing awkwardly in her living room, we said good-bye and left.

The very next week, Joy Dawson felt she should write Kalafi one more letter. It arrived, we learned later, the day before Kalafi planned a party complete with drugs. Kalafi picked up Joy's letter at the post office, took it to his car, and tore it open.

Suddenly God spoke to him. Kalafi could hear Him with his natural ears, and he began sweating all over.

"Kalafi," the Lord said tenderly, "living the Christian life is difficult. There is only one thing harder—that's not being a Christian. The price that you pay to follow Me is far less than the price you'll have to pay not to follow Me."

Kalafi found the nearest phone booth and called me on the Big Island. He contacted the Dawsons and prayed with them for hours, ending five months of separation from God. Then he came back to Hawaii. I sensed he needed time to heal. At my encouragement, he enrolled in the University of Hawaii on the other side of the Big Island. In his spare time, Kalafi started a landscape business, which was soon flourishing. Kalafi never did things by halves!

He told me on a visit to our side of the island that he never expected to have a ministry again. "It'll be enough if Jesus forgives me," he said. "I just need to *be* for a while, not do."

Watching Kalafi's progress over the next year and a half meant at times watching him fall backward. Kalafi and Tapu tried to get back together, but the effort failed. They called it quits and were divorced. Kalafi began drinking a bit again.

When I confronted him, he asked me to let him alone. Shortly afterward, we learned that he had remarried. Leda, his new wife, was not a Christian.

All the while, we were having to walk such a tightrope, choosing where to confront and where to give a loose rein. Kalafi had come into YWAM before our training schools had started, so he had not experienced that discipline before being thrust into leadership. In a way, what we were going through now was an individualized crash course.

"The only thing is," I said to Dar one night when we were stretched out on the floor in our living room interceding for Kalafi, "I sometimes wonder if he will pass the course."

One special, special day, nine months after we had heard that Kalafi had remarried, I received a telephone call.

"Could Leda and I come over for a visit with you?" Kalafi asked.

Could they come over? Need he ask? Nothing would thrill our hearts more. "Yes, yes," I said. "Friday night?"

So Kalafi and Leda, who was pregnant, arrived for dinner. Joy Dawson had been teaching at our school on the Big Island, and this was her last evening with us. After our meal Joy took Kalafi aside while Dar talked to Leda. Like a flower exposed to sunlight, Leda immediately opened up to receive Jesus. We were so excited.

I looked across the room where Joy was in earnest conversation with Kalafi. I could see by his hunched shoulders and furrowed brow that he was weighing his total surrender to God. As he left that night, I knew Kalafi's destiny was still hanging in the balance. He knew too much of God and had experienced too much of His power and working in his life to ever live in mediocrity.

A few weeks later Kalafi called again. This time, he asked if he could see me privately.

I saw to my relief, as Kalafi sat with head bowed and hands folded, that he was ready to make a clear-cut choice to obey God wholeheartedly. He poured out hurts and guilt that he had been harboring for years. It was a sad, familiar tale of lust and pride, which he had never been able to confess fully. We both wept. As I stood beside Kalafi to pray with him, I knew that here, in spite of the struggles, was a young man God wanted to use.

Kalafi decided that he had to write letters to all of the churches and YWAM bases where he had ministered over the years, telling them frankly of his sins and asking for forgiveness. He also wrote to Tapu, asking her forgiveness, and to his own family back in Tonga.

Then one of the more intriguing forms of guidance began to take place. Kalafi's landscaping business suddenly went sour.

Kalafi had taken on two major jobs, but now, unexplainably, he met delay after delay. A bulldozer would break down. He would hire another, and in an hour or two it too would break down. After five such mishaps, Kalafi began to wonder if maybe God wasn't trying to tell him something! Then a friend called, inviting Kalafi to speak at a Saturday night Bible study class in a nearby church. At first he did not want to go, but Leda encouraged him.

"They're not asking you to preach, Kalafi. They just want you to tell what's been happening."

Finally he accepted and went to speak at the Bible study. That Saturday night he stood in the sanctuary of this church, telling how he had tried to walk away from the Lord, how he had committed adultery, how his marriage had broken up, and how God was now leading him back.

As he spoke, Kalafi began to weep. To his amazement, a man in the first row fell to his knees beside his chair. Then another did the same. People all over the church were weeping. Several gave their lives to Jesus that night, and others had their broken marriages restored.

After that powerful night, Kalafi knew God was giving him back his ministry. He and Leda soon began to visit us regularly on Friday nights. They were always brimming with news. Kalafi finally got the message from the broken-down bulldozers and gave up his business. He and Leda were now living on whatever God provided. They began conducting a Christian fellowship every Friday night, leading people to Christ and seeing broken bodies and minds mended by the power of the Gospel.

I wondered about Kalafi's ministry after his divorce and remarriage. It seemed clear to me that although divorce was not in God's perfect plan, it was not the unpardonable sin, either. It was God who had restored Kalafi's ministry. If being perfectly at the heart of His will were the criterion for ministry, how many of us would qualify? Thankfully, even when we fail, God does not take back His gifts and callings.

It was exciting to watch Kalafi come back to fruitfulness in the Lord's work. At the same time, we were watching the campus of our future university slowly emerge from beneath the tropical overgrowth.

To be honest, with all that was going on, I'd just about forgotten the one remaining element in that all-night seeking session we'd held in Kaneohe nearly four years ago. Those prophecies had also included seeing a ship anchored in Kona Bay. That, however, was a suppression of memory that wasn't going to last long.

SEVENTEEN

Don't Give Up the Ship

ONE day, about two months after Dar and I moved into our rooms at the hotel in Kona, I was on a trip visiting with Don Stephens.

"Loren," Don said, "I wonder if God might not be stirring up the ship vision again."

My reaction was immediate. "Oh no, not another ship!" I mumbled under my breath. That would be two major projects at the same time—the university and the ship.

Thankfully, Don didn't hear my mumbling. He went on to describe a ship he had located in Venice, Italy. "It's called the *Victoria*," Don said, his eyes alive. "I've taken several European YWAMers to see it, though I sometimes wonder why. It is a huge old thing, and it has no lights. The generator isn't even running. It's just a big eleven-thousand-ton passenger liner dead in the water.

"But, Loren," Don ran on excitedly, "the ship could be bought for a song precisely because it is in such bad shape. There'd be lots of repairs, but we could handle that, don't you think?"

I'm afraid I said nothing at all.

"Well," Don finished lamely, dampened by my lack of response, "there was something special about the *Victoria*...."

Looking for something to say, I asked, "What color is the ship, Don?"

"White," he replied.

For the first time since this conversation began, my heart skipped a beat. The ship we'd "seen" in the bay in our all-night prayer meeting in Kaneohe...that ship was white, too.

About two months later, a man came to the Big Island and asked around until he found out where we lived. He was in my office at the hotel now, looking out over the freshly landscaped tropical foliage.

"Paul Ainsworth's my name. From Toronto."

He began to shift uneasily on the folding canvas chair. I smiled, trying to put him at ease. "Frankly, sir," Mr. Ainsworth went on, "I don't really know why I'm here, except that I've had a very strange experience, and somehow it may involve you. You see, sir, I've...well...I've had a vision."

I was becoming interested, and Mr. Ainsworth stumbled on. He told me how a few days earlier he had been at a prayer meeting in Toronto. All of a sudden, in front of his eyes he saw a map of the South Pacific. He saw a large white ship coming across his vision. The ship seemed to be sailing from the Hawaiian Islands, heading south.

I was suddenly very interested.

"I could read the names of the islands on the map," Mr. Ainsworth said. "Someone in the prayer meeting got out an atlas and started following the route I was describing in my vision. Everything matched."

I was now sitting on the very edge of my own canvas chair. Mr. Ainsworth's next words sent chills through me. "As the ship moved through the Pacific," he said, "a revival broke out. Thousands of South Sea Islanders came to Jesus, and then they themselves became evangelists. They went into Southeast Asia, right up into India, and on into China. Millions came to know the Lord."

The vision had lasted for two hours, Paul Ainsworth said, and some of the details he told me didn't seem to apply to us.

"What do you want me to do now, Lord?" he had asked God. The Lord said, "Go to Hawaii." Mr. Ainsworth knew no one in Hawaii, but in obedience he made travel plans. Before he left, a friend handed him a piece of paper, saying, "This man may help you. He lives in Hawaii." Paul Ainsworth opened the note on the plane. All it said was *Loren Cunningham*.

I could hardly believe what I was hearing. Mr. Ainsworth was now studying my face, waiting, no doubt, for some indication that this all made sense. I was near tears myself, but I walked over and picked up the plaque my mother had given me. I showed it to him and then had the unusual pleasure of telling this obedient man our entire story. We both started to laugh the way I have seen Polynesians laugh, out of sheer nervousness. Mother's plaque, of course, said, "Don't Give Up the Ship."

Everything was happening too quickly and too spectacularly, and the amazing series of events was not over yet. After Mr. Ainsworth's visit, Darlene received a letter from an old friend who spent much time in intercession for YWAM. She wrote, "The Lord told me you and Loren are giving birth to twins. Not literally, I'm sure. I believe the twins are ministries. One is the ship. I'm not sure what the other one is...."

It seemed everywhere we turned, we were hearing about twins! Some could hardly be called divine guidance, but they were fun to think about anyhow. My mind ran back to the delightful day, a few months earlier, when Jimmy and Jannie finally had a family after eleven years of marriage. We were all surprised when Jannie gave birth to identical twin boys, born seven minutes apart on 7-7-77. It did seem that God was saying something to us about twins.

After such a stunning series of Bible-story-like encouragements, we had to plunge ahead with negotiations for the purchase of the *Victoria*. I suppose God had to be so overwhelmingly obvious with me because He knew I might give up otherwise. I had to be absolutely sure that He was resurrecting our vision. And as I prayed about moving forward, I wondered: How is He ever going to release enough money to accomplish such a mission?

Three months after Don first spoke to me about it, we decided to begin negotiations with the owners of the *Victoria*. I couldn't help but laugh at the contrast between talking deposits and payouts and escrows on the one hand and, on the other, watching Dar wash our dishes in the bathroom sink at our hotel room.

Don sent me a picture of the ship, along with a diagram of the vessel. But I have to admit that after the experience with the *Maori*, I put the diagram in a drawer.

Then a month later, in April 1978, I flew to Venice to meet with Don. It was a two-purpose visit. Four hundred YWAMers were here talking to people about Jesus on the streets of Venice. They were living in a campground on the outskirts of the city. But, of course, I was especially interested in Venice because that was where the *Victoria* was berthed.

As Don drove me from the airport, he updated me on the negotiations. The owners were considering our offer, submitted a month earlier, and had even sought government approval for the sale if they should decide to go ahead.

"These people did not take us seriously at first," Don said as we snaked through traffic, "and I can't blame them. We're so naive about shipping, we had to ask them which questions to ask. We were embarrassed to give our address, care of a campground!"

We drove down the causeway linking Venice to the mainland and then pulled off the road. Don pointed toward the dockside cranes.

"There she is."

In spite of myself, I must admit my heart raced. There she lay with her orange and black smokestack. "And the symbol on the stack," Don was saying, "is the lion of St. Mark the evangelist, patron saint of Venice. Interesting, no?"

I'm not sure that Don understood my reluctance, but I did not want to go aboard the ship right then. The trouble was that I might become too excited. After the experience with the *Maori*, the last thing I wanted to do was exalt another piece of metal.

But I was certainly open to letting the Lord work through Don and the other men. For me personally, it was a matter of keeping a balance between the spiritual caution I'd learned from the *Maori* and the boldness I'd gained from hearing Paul Ainsworth's vision.

So I encouraged Don to go ahead. When he related the overwhelming task to be done, I could only say, "Don, let's break the job down into small units so we can handle it. God never expects us to take more than one step at a time."

I went home with a mixture of excitement and concern. Darlene and I kept coming back to the same question: "Is that really You, Lord?" We had seen before at times of great turning points that it helps to ask ourselves, "How much of the supernatural is there in the guidance we are receiving?" We had not been asking for signs, nor had we been seeking the spectacular, but signs and spectacular coincidences had been occurring one after another. It seemed spiritual foolishness not to pay attention! God was probably saying, "This is the way, walk in it."

So Don went ahead with the negotiations. A month later he telephoned from Venice all excited. The ship owners had approved our offer; government authorities were in accord.

"You should have seen us, Loren!" Don reported. "Everybody wanted to go down for the signing. Five of us crowded into a tiny French Renault 4 and drove out of a campground to sign for a ship!"

So we had our contract. We scraped up money for the down payment from funds raised within YWAM. But something other than money was being released here, something that was at the very heart of our original concept of Youth With A Mission.

One of the most trustworthy tests for valid guidance is this: Does it bring the people who are involved one step closer to freedom and maturity in the Lord? If this is not so, the guidance is probably suspect. If the guidance moves people into a deeper relationship with the Lord, then the direction is probably from God. In this particular instance, Don Stephens was the principal person being released. He had proven himself in Munich, and now he was being given a far tougher mission.

All the while, like the image through binoculars that is coming into focus, our university concept was becoming clearer. Dr. Howard Malmstadt, the professor who had come to our doorstep, had indeed stayed on, just as God had indicated. He and I now spent hours lying on the blue carpet of our apartment, praying and planning and brainstorming. Howard introduced me to an architect who peppered us with questions about the relationship-oriented lifestyle plans for U of N. We explained to him that students, staff, visiting teachers, and their families would all live together in villages, with 280 people in each village. We wanted this type of living arrangement because most of the students would be Asian and Pacific Islanders who lived in villages at home. We told the architect about the colleges that were forming around the "mind molders," those areas that shape a society and culture. The campus needed to be designed to encourage a live-learn environment within these colleges. Our architect was excited by the challenge. He flew back to the mainland and began to draw up the campus design, donating it as a labor of love.

I worried a lot about the size of the two commitments we were facing. I worried about the money to finance such an undertaking, of course, but that wasn't my real concern.

Our efforts at being led by the Lord had revealed a danger area in guidance. Divine guidance is so heady, so spectacular, that there is the risk of glory attaching itself to the work rather than to the Lord. We'd made that mistake with the *Maori,* and we were determined not to let it happen again!

But a second danger area showed up now. When God guides us, He is taking a risk, too. If we make the wrong choices, we can end up robbing Him not only of His glory but also of His rightful first *attention.*

Without realizing it, I was about to head into this second danger zone. Ever since Munich, we'd made an effort to be at major international sporting events. They were miniature worlds, often giving us opportunities to meet people from "closed" countries. One such event was the World Cup soccer games to be held over a four-week period in Argentina in June 1978, only eight weeks away. I made preparations to go, satisfied that God wanted me there.

Then, shortly before my departure for the World Cup, a friend phoned from the mainland.

"Loren, I've got the best news. I've met a real estate developer who wants to give a lot of money for a Christian university," he said excitedly. "He'd like to meet with you. He's in Denver."

A large donation like this could get the university going sooner than we thought! I'd be a day or two late getting to the World Cup, maybe, but on the other hand...

"I'll swing by and visit him on my way to Argentina," I said, trying to keep my voice calm.

So on the day I was supposed to fly to Buenos Aires, I flew instead to Denver. By the time I finally arrived in Argentina after some delays, the games were two-thirds through.

I met with the teams and tried to make up for lost time with extra enthusiasm. But the respectful, polite mood of the young people was like that of a youngster playing in the finals of a high school football season, only to have Dad show up in the third quarter because he'd been at an important meeting. The mood of our staff, too, worried me. When I explained where I'd been, no one was impressed. The World Cup was the event we'd all been led to, and though no one said so outright, I knew that I had some thinking to do.

That night—very late—in my room in the school in Buenos Aires where seven hundred of us were being housed, I began to think about the guidance factors involved in this experience.

I had no doubt in my mind that the university was a dream dear to the heart of God. It was a fresh way of sending waves of young people into new mission fields, the mind-molding centers of our society. But the *Maori* had been a tool close to the heart of God, too. I still believed that. Yet He let the ship die because it was becoming a glorious thing all in itself.

With the university, God's call for our attention was threatened in an even more serious way. God had told me to be in Argentina. I heard the directions clearly. But I ended up chasing after money instead. That is when I first wished I had a wall-hanging that said, *Guidance is first of all a relationship with the Guide*. The first goal of guidance is to lead us into a closer relationship with Jesus. All other goals should be subservient to that.

We have to be especially watchful when He is leading us toward *tools*, such as a ship or a university. There is nothing wrong with tools. But it's a sad day if the tools ever supersede the Lord Himself.

EIGHTEEN ⤸

"Doesn't Anybody Care?"

DON Stephens called Dar and me late one evening seven months after we began negotiating for the *Victoria*. Dar had managed in the year we'd been in our apartment at the Kona hotel to make the three rooms into a home. She was beginning to accumulate a chair here, a lamp there.

"Well, Loren, it's done," Don's voice came in over the satellite telephone. He seemed excited, and yet strangely subdued.

"We have a ship?" I asked. Dar perked up from across the room. For months now, money had been coming in with encouraging regularity. It was, we believed, a major part of our guidance.

"We have a ship. She's not seaworthy, but she's ours. The owners waited until the last dollar was in before they let the ship go."

Don said they'd be holding a candlelight thanksgiving feast in the ship's dining room; then they'd go to the afterdeck to lower the ensign and replace it with our own.

"Of course our problems have just begun, Loren," Don said. No wonder he seemed both excited and subdued. "Sooner or later, we'll have to leave Venice because we have a nonunion crew. We'll have to be towed somewhere for dry docking. Probably Greece."

"Don," I said, feeling that I needed to shift the conversation, "what do you think of the new name by now?"

"The *Anastasis*?" That was the name we'd liked. "Yes, it seems right."

"The *Anastasis* it is, then," I said, looking at Dar, who was listening to one side of the phone conversation, glad that she was smiling her agreement.

Anastasis is the Greek word for resurrection.

One of the difficulties of being led by the Lord is keeping perspective. As divine guidance begins to unfold, it always seems to come with hard, gritty work. Gone is the thrill of the original leading. Ahead, still, is the excitement of seeing the fruit of this same leading. All that's left in between is mind-numbing, muscle-straining labor. It is in this interim period that the Perspective Principle becomes so important.

It was June 1979, and a year had passed since I had first seen "our" ship. Now, as my Alitalia flight circled the canals of Venice, I craned my neck to catch a glimpse of the *Anastasis*. Some sixty of us were gathering in Venice. Don needed to see as many of the YWAM leaders from around the world as possible so that we could reassure him of our support. And we needed to rekindle our vision of a ship going out in Jesus' name.

My eyes scanned the sparkling waters. There she lay in the glare of the Venetian sun—still with her rather shabby coat of white paint, but now with a blue and green smokestack. Half an hour later, a sleek water taxi was bouncing over the harbor toward our ship. I could pick out the freshly painted YWAM logo on the smokestack. We rounded the stem to come alongside the gangplank. The old name had been painted over, and now, emblazoned across the stem in black letters, was the word *Anastasis*.

As I stepped on deck, Don and his volunteer workers—most of whom were quite young—greeted me warmly. I had been reluctant to come aboard until we knew there was no turning back, still determined not to glorify a mere tool in God's kingdom. But now I was glad to be here, taking the tour of the 522-foot vessel, its large dining rooms, forward lounge, small hospital unit, and five large cargo holds. I could see where young volunteers had put in countless hours scraping, sanding, repairing, and painting. The galley alone, Don said, had taken twenty-five young people three weeks to clean.

By now other leaders were coming on board. Sixty of us gathered on the promenade deck, where passengers had formerly sunbathed during long ocean voyages. Don began to tell us of the complexities of towing the ship to Athens and preparing her for operation. We prayed over these problems, putting the Perspective Principle to work by recalling both the original vision and the future potential of a ship as an evangelistic and mercy ministry tool. We would need this confirmation to carry us through the long hard months ahead.

The visit to the *Anastasis* was over. As our launch pulled away, I think all of us felt a renewed understanding of God's yearning for His people to be involved in mercy ministry. What pleased me was that the next step thrusting YWAM into ministering to these needs came from a brand-new generation, the twenty-seven-year-old son of Jim and Joy Dawson.

"Loren," John Dawson said to me back in the States, "God has been speaking to me…and I think His message is for all of us in YWAM."

John had my attention instantly. This young man had lots of family experience hearing the voice of God. He went on to relate how he had recently read an article in *Time* magazine about refugees fleeing Vietnam.

"Loren," John said, "these 'Boat People' pay outrageous sums for leaky tubs to try to get out of Vietnam. Then they are pirated and shot, or left adrift on rafts." Nobody wanted to help these people. John described the overcrowded refugee camps in neighboring countries. "Loren, I couldn't get away from the title of the article, 'Doesn't Anyone Care?' This is the world's question to the Body of Christ. That's how God must feel about these people. He's sobbing, 'Doesn't anyone care?'"

John's challenge began to haunt me. Was his concern at last the beginning of the mercy missions I had envisioned ever since Hurricane Cleo fifteen years earlier?

I decided to have a look for myself. Taking a few other YWAM leaders, I went to Hong Kong and then to Thailand. The first refugee camp we visited was in Hong Kong. No magazine articles could prepare our eyes and ears—or nose— for the shock of that scene in Jubilee Camp.

The smell came first. The putrid stench of raw human waste hit us before we entered the place. As we walked in the main entrance into an inner passageway, we found the source. The lower floor of the building was eight inches deep in human excrement and waste water. We picked our way around the perimeter as best we could as camp officials pointed to some broken sewer pipes along the side of the wall. There was not enough money to hire a plumber from the city, and no one there was qualified or willing to tackle the huge mess.

Jubilee Camp was a former police barracks designed to hold nine hundred. Now the condemned structure held eight thousand. The government simply had no other place to put the overwhelming number of refugees. Each room held wall-to-wall bunks, three high, with several families living in each tier. One family would occupy two bunks: not just for sleeping, but for everything, including cooking. The doctors of the camp, pitifully overworked, told how every day they would treat the concussions of small children who had fallen from high bunks in their sleep.

Already my mind was busy thinking of the possibilities of helping. Did we have to wait? We could bring workers here even before the *Anastasis* was under sail. We could help clean up the mess, help care for the sick, and also have a chance to share the message of Jesus with these people—that He cared about their suffering and wanted to do something about it. We would be sharing His love with one hand and His truth with the other.

The concern and strange excitement that we felt in Hong Kong we also felt in Thailand. I watched a Hmong mother hold out the skeletal frame of a baby boy with his too-large head lolling backward. Regrettably food had come to him too late. My stomach knotted as I heard the rattle in his tiny throat. My eyes filled with tears as he drew his last shuddering breath and his mother clasped his lifeless body to her. *Where?* I screamed inside of myself, *Where is the Church of Jesus Christ?*

A moment later I looked into the eyes of a youthful Khmer Rouge soldier. He might have been one of those who had thrown a baby into the air and caught him on the point of his bayonet. The young man's eyes were vacant, gaping portholes into hell itself. But Jesus had died for this man, too. Through an interpreter, I spoke with twelve hundred of the Khmer Rouge in that camp. Many listened intently to our account of God's love, forgiveness, and call to repentance.

Two dozen men came apart with me to pray, at no little risk to their own safety.

When I returned to Kona I felt a deep heaviness, but I also felt great excitement and a sense of completion. At last we were coming full circle with our ministry of mercy at YWAM. The long-awaited twins of the Good News—an ever deeper love of God and, its identical counterpart, an ever deeper love for our neighbor—were at last really being brought into the world.

Within weeks we had young people out working in the refugee camps. Gary Stephens (Don's younger brother) led a group of thirty into Jubilee Camp. The YWAMers did what even the refugees had been unwilling to do: They shoveled out all the human waste, repaired the broken sewage pipes, and fixed the toilets. Gary reported back that the refugees marveled at what they saw in our workers. Here were young people who were paying their own way to come and do a job no one else would consider. The YWAMers had their attention, all right! Time after time they were given the opening they had hoped for: They were asked why they had come.

Soon the team had permission from camp officials to start a school, hold Bible study classes, and offer counseling.

Then an amazing thing happened. It seemed as though God had been waiting for this particular obedience to open His storehouse. As word spread of our finally released emphasis on the second twin—the practical demonstration of our love toward our neighbor—workers streamed to join our ranks. It was as if we had opened a door against which hundreds of young men and women had been pressed, waiting to pour through. More experienced people started to join our work, too: doctors, nurses, and technical experts, as well as people willing to roll bandages or teach refugee youths. Soon we found a dozen opportunities—vocational rehabilitation, cottage industries, food and clothing distribution, English classes, and cultural reorientation for those headed for a new life in another country. And all the while, with both our actions and our words, we were spreading the Gospel, leading people to their heavenly Father.

The blessings of God flowed elsewhere as well. Kalafi was doing well in his newly regained ministry. The old fire was back, along with a new tenderness, gained after his own fall. Kalafi had started schools in Honolulu, Singapore, and Jakarta, training young evangelists. Stories drifted back of hundreds being saved and of healings—a deaf girl instantly hearing in Malaysia, an old crippled Muslim in Indonesia running and jumping after Kalafi prayed for him—and of churches being formed in unreached villages.

We positively glowed over these reports that showed Kalafi's complete restoration.

God was heaping blessings on top of blessings now. *Like Jim and Jannie's story*, I smiled to myself. They had waited eleven years for a family, and then their twins were born. Now they also had a third boy—an added, special gift.

And that's the way it was in YWAM as well. All over the world, God was adding more and more gifts, multiplying releases.

One leader, Al Akimoff, sent two thousand people into the Soviet Union in 1980 to proclaim the Gospel. Another man, Floyd McClung, and his family moved in among the prostitutes, male and female, of the Red Light District of Amsterdam. Other men were becoming responsible for different zones of the world: Africa, North and South America. The multiplication principle was at work, too: YWAMers in Brazil reported that young people trained in our Schools of

Evangelism were now themselves pushing into their own frontiers, going up the Amazon to reach isolated Indian tribes with the Gospel.

And our work? Darlene's and mine? As we had foreseen when we moved to Hawaii, our attention was turning toward Asia. We visited teams, joining in the evangelism, giving training to our growing family of eighteen hundred full-time workers. I still carried the weight of my own home base at Kona, believing firmly that the formation of a university was a vision dear to God's heart. But instead of waiting for a campus and buildings, we started *where we were*. The buildings were only tools, after all.

So the University of the Nations began. We rented a room here, a meeting hall there, an apartment somewhere else, and began teaching.

In the meantime, our other twin ministry was still very much alive. As I would be discovering shortly.

NINETEEN ⟋

A Fish Story

HALFWAY around the world, my friend Don Stephens and his team of 175 crew and students were trying to get the *Anastasis* ready to sail under her own steam. Don called me from Athens in early 1981. I was sitting on the lanai of our home at the school, looking out through the coconut palms toward the blueness of the bay. I could picture Don in Athens, calling from some anonymous phone booth. He briefed me on how his people were holding up.

"They are the real heroes, Loren," Don said, bragging as he always did about his team. His young men and women had to worm their way into the stinking bilge of the ship to clean it. For long hours every day they scrubbed, scoured, polished, and painted. And they accomplished all of this hard work with so little money that they could buy generator oil for only a few hours of electricity at a time. Their food was mostly peanut butter and rice and beans. The Athens port authorities would not let them live on board, so they stayed in an old hotel that had been damaged in a recent earthquake. But just as in Hawaii we had decided not to wait on a tool (the buildings and campus) before obeying God's call to start the university, so also Don and his team in Athens decided not to wait for their tool (the ship) before obeying God's call to a mercy ministry. At every opportunity, Don's team members were out helping Greek people suffering from the earthquake. They also were hard at work every day taking the Gospel onto the streets right where they were.

I was pleased at what I was hearing. "Don," I said, "we're finally getting the message, aren't we? God wants us to focus our attention on His call, not on His tools."

All of YWAM began to help in the huge finances needed for the ship itself. But the young people under Don and Deyon continued to be responsible for their own support, usually through regular, nonbegging, informative letters to folks back home. Very often the provision had an air of mystery about it. The kids would write to one person and get back a letter of encouragement from someone else—often someone they'd never heard of. Very often, funds would come in from a totally unexpected direction.

The closer the *Anastasis* came to being seaworthy, the more often Don insisted on pulling back to basics. Why were the young people willing to crawl between the plates of the ship to clean it out? Because they were evangelists. They were already asking God for a huge harvest, thousands upon thousands of people who would be brought into His kingdom, and thousands more who would be helped through acts of mercy. In preparation for this releasing, Don became intrigued by the link between prayer and fasting, guidance, and a good harvest. Jesus, after all, began His incredibly fruitful ministry after the wilderness fast. Perhaps the ship team should do the same!

So Don and Deyon and their 175 team members began a forty-day fast, rotating commitment so that at all times several people were doing the spiritual work of fasting and praying. I was fascinated by their earnestness to start this new ministry on the right foundation. I remembered the same kind of fasting prayer in the Dawsons' New Zealand home immediately before the substantial release of workers for YWAM.

The forty-day spiritual discipline in Athens was just about over. One day the telephone rang. It was Don.

"Loren, are you ready?"

"Ready!" I could tell from the lightness in Don's voice that the news was good.

"Just make notes, good friend," Don said. "As soon as we began to see what was happening, we took very accurate account, and these figures are not exaggerated by even one fish. Listen to this." And then Don told the story of what happened as the crew was fasting and praying to be guided toward an abundant harvest.

One of the ship's crew was walking along the beach near the hotel where the team lived. Suddenly he saw twelve medium-sized fish jump over the rocks into a shallow tidal pool right at his feet. He caught them and ran to the hotel to show the others. It was a big enough catch that a few staffers were able to have a fish fry to supplement their rice that night. A few days later, a large tuna jumped out of the sea onto the beach. This time, more YWAMers got to eat a portion with their evening meal.

Again, a few days later, one of our young team members from Dallas, Texas, was seated on the rocks by the sea, having her quiet time. Suddenly fish began to jump. She whooped and shouted. Local Greek families saw what was happening and ran up to catch the fish, too. Becky gathered 210 fish, and the Greek families took two or three times that much home.

But the biggest fish story was yet to come.

"Just last Tuesday, Loren, at eight in the morning, the fish began jumping again!" Don and Deyon and the others ran down to the sea shouting. For 150 yards downshore they could see fish leaping onto land. They ran back to the hotel and grabbed every container they could find—plastic buckets, dishpans, large bags. "Our crew spent forty-five minutes gathering fish as fast as we could," Don said. What was causing them to leap up on the shore that way? Nobody knew. Their Greek friends had never seen anything like it. They said, "God is with these people."

When the great fishing party was over, they counted what they had been given in this unusual way. "Loren, you won't believe how many!" Don said. "There were 8,301—over one ton of fish, Loren! You can imagine the praise session we had right there on the beach. This was the encouragement we needed that the ministry of the *Anastasis* is going to be very, very special indeed."

Just as suddenly as the fish began to jump, signaling an abundant harvest for the *Anastasis*' mercy ministry, so was the final money released to pay for the technical work being done by the shipyard. Funds came in from all over the world. Hundreds of thousands of additional dollars were given sacrificially by YWAMers themselves and by groups such as 100 Huntley Street, 700 Club, PTL Club, the Billy Graham Evangelistic Association, David Wilkerson Youth Crusades, and Last Days Ministries.

God's overwhelming supply of funds to finish the work left no doubt about it. The ship ministry was in the process of being born.

And what about the University of the Nations? We had at last found long-term financing. Even so, a casual observer strolling around the old grounds of the Pacific Empress Hotel would hardly call this a university. We continued to press ahead anyhow. We dared not wait, in part because of a specific word given us by an obstetrician friend, who warned during one of our times of prayer for guidance that in the birth of twins, the pregnancy had to be treated as *one*. When one twin is born, the other must follow very rapidly, or the life of the mother and the second twin will be jeopardized. He repeated again and again: We *must* see the second twin, U of N, born shortly, or both the mother, YWAM, and the second twin would die.

This word encouraged us to continue our plans with or without buildings and a campus. Again, our early history followed in the grand tradition of another great center of learning. Oxford University, for instance, for years was an unglamorous collection of teachers and students getting together in whatever facilities they could find.

In Kona we had a few disciplines starting up already, including counseling, psychology training (from a biblical base), paramedical training, preschool teacher training, science, technology geared to the Third World, as well as schools of biblical study, missiology, and church ministry. These colleges-in-embryo were sprinkled along the Kona Coast in whatever locations we could find.

The two ministries now were tracking each other closely. News of the firstborn was good. The *Anastasis'* sea trials in Athens had gone off without a hitch. Final procedures were under way for registering the vessel under the flag of Malta. This registration would allow us to sail with a nonunion international crew. Since we planned to have the crew of the *Anastasis* follow the usual YWAM pattern of depending on God for their own financial support, we could hardly comply with regulations of countries such as Italy, where only unionized crews were recognized.

The great day for launching this new ministry finally came.

The *Anastasis* pulled up anchor and sailed from Greece on July 7, 1982. Was it an accident that that day was the fifth birthday of Jim and Jannie's twins?

The ship was on its way to California. Darlene and I and Karen and David, now ages fourteen and eleven, were in L.A. for the welcoming ceremony for the *Anastasis*. What a special occasion! The ship was steaming into the very city where YWAM had gotten its start.

I thought of how much had happened in the twenty-two years since we began with a dream in a bedroom office. It had been a bumpy beginning. But so much had come full circle. I smiled as I recalled a recent meeting with my former leader in the Assemblies of God. I had told Thomas Zimmerman how much I loved and appreciated him, thanking him for the role he had played at a crucial time in my life. Perhaps without even realizing it, he had helped me solidify the vision God had given me—that He wanted the waves of young people to go out from *every* denomination, not just my own. Before we parted, we both agreed it would be good for him to come speak at our school in Kona in the near future. I shook his hand and said, "Thank you, Brother Zimmerman." He was indeed a dear brother.

Now I was standing among two thousand people from every sort of church and denomination who had come to Berth 51 in Los Angeles Harbor to celebrate the ship's arrival. I found it interesting that I was standing there almost as a spectator. Don had very capably brought this vision, which I had received eighteen years before, to reality. His growth in leadership, and then mentoring all those who had helped in birthing this dream, was what multiplication was all about.

Melody Green, the widow of popular singer Keith Green, recently killed in an air crash, spoke from our portable stage about Keith's great desire to see the *Anastasis* ministry

launched. Then over a loudspeaker came a taped recording
of Keith singing, "Holy, Holy, Holy!" As his voice filled
Berth 51, our huge white ship pulled into view and steamed
slowly to dockside. People picked up on Keith's theme:

> Holy, Holy, Holy,
> Lord God Almighty!
> Early in the morning,
> Our song shall rise to Thee!

I looked around me. Everywhere people were either smiling or rejoicing or weeping as they sang about the Lord. I
nudged Darlene.

"What a difference," I whispered.

"Difference?"

"Between this scene, praising God the way we are, and
that horrible vision nine years ago when I saw our leaders
shouting in excitement over a ship but ignoring Jesus in the
shadows."

"You're right," Darlene said. She took my hand. "This is
what hearing God's voice is all about, isn't it? Getting to
know Him better!"

TWENTY

Getting to Know Him Better

IT WAS springtime and we were in Kona. For weeks bulldozers had been rumbling over the property—to the utter delight of David, now twelve years old—rooting out boulders and leveling sites for the first buildings of the University of the Nations.

A lot had happened in the eight months since the official welcoming at Berth 51 in Los Angeles. The *Anastasis* had sailed to the South Pacific, helping the poor and needy in many ports of call.

Our multiplication principle was strongly at work. Each of our YWAM missionaries was a potential multiplier, too. Many, like Jim Rogers, Leland Paris, Floyd McClung, Don Stephens, and Kalafi Moala, now headed work of their own within YWAM. To see the principle of multiplication happening in the lives of those I respected and had worked with gave me the greatest satisfaction. God had multiplied the vision by thousands. Along the way, I had stumblingly learned how to hear His voice, and even more stumblingly, I was learning to obey Him. Now if each of these new missionaries could do the same, using our early mistakes and successes as steppingstones, what power would be released!

That power we had prayed for was already being released. In May 1983 our key leaders from around the world poured into Kona for our annual strategy conference. In one room were clustered some of my dearest friends, my comrades. They took turns sharing what God had been doing in their lives. We learned what YWAM expected to accomplish for the year:

- At our present rate, by December 1983, we would have ministered in 193 of the 223 countries on earth.
- We would have at least fifteen thousand short-term volunteers go out for the year.
- We would have thirty-eight hundred full-time workers by December 1983; one-fourth of these would be from the Third World.
- We would have 113 permanent bases and seventy schools located in forty nations by the end of the year.
- We could now go with a ship full of supplies to areas where there was special need. Besides the ship's work, victims of war and poverty were being helped in twelve countries on five continents.
- In Thailand alone, YWAMers taught seven hundred refugee children every day.
- In 1982, we gave new clothes to thirty thousand refugees.
- In one year, one thousand young evangelists from thirty different countries were sent to the Soviet Union.
- Every month, YWAMers in Hollywood handled two thousand calls from runaways, many of whom were teenage boy and girl prostitutes.

We heard how our young missionaries were going out to Himalayan kingdoms...up the Amazon...to punk rockers in Japan...staging street dramas in France...feeding Hong Kong squatters...helping starving African tribesmen...giving medical aid in war-torn Lebanon...and taking a Bible to every home in many Mexican cities. As my friends told what their teams were doing in each area, I felt my excitement rising like the waves. I remembered my first trip to Africa as a young man, when I was the first missionary ever to talk to a leathery chief about the Great God who made us all. But I also recalled leaving the area by air and seeing smoke trailing upward from a thousand fires, each one representing an unreached village! I recalled being stunned at the enormity of the mandate: *Go ye into all the world and preach the Gospel to every creature.* Yet the smoke of African villages paled beside the multitudes of Asia, where forty thousand people could live in one high-rise apartment complex, where sixty percent of the world's people lived, and where almost none had heard of Jesus Christ!

We were sending out fifteen thousand workers a year, but they were only a fraction of what was needed. If each of these workers reached one hundred people, that would be only one and a half million out of the four billion on earth at the time! The laborers were still few, very few. Only God was great enough to fulfill the vision of the waves and see every person on earth receive a personal message of His love for them.

On the last evening of the strategy conference, we all went out for a dedication of the site of the university, scrambling over raw earth that had been roughly leveled by the bulldozers.

We stood in a circle around the site where the Plaza of Nations would be. The sun was setting over the blue Pacific in the background. I looked at the flags of some of the nations where we were working. As they fluttered against a darkening cobalt sky, I could see the waves of young people going out. I had originally dreamed of a thousand. I could now imagine hundreds of thousands going out, until every continent was covered by people bringing the twin-natured message of the Gospel: Love the Lord with all your heart, and love your neighbor as yourself.

Only one final part of the vision remained, and that would take place in just seven months.

It was Saturday morning, December 17, 1983. As the sun rose from the mountains of Hawaii, the final symbolic touch-stone for our entire story was about to take place.

Darlene and I, Karen and David, Mom and Dad, and Darlene's parents were among the two thousand who were eagerly scanning the water. Small children were perched on parents' shoulders. Then, slowly, a white ship appeared on the horizon. Some started clapping. There were shouts— "Glory!" "Praise God!" Outrigger canoes hurried out to meet her as the music of a Hawaiian hymn rose above the bay.

Ten years before, when we had had the amazing experience of the Lord's foretelling the future while teenagers prayed together right here in the Hawaiian Islands, we had seen a great white ship steaming into port. Even then we had known—although it defied all logic—that this was a vision of our mercy missions ship sailing into the harbor at Kona.

And here she was. The *Anastasis*. The Resurrection. Put your dreams on the altar. They will be resurrected into something even grander.

How can I possibly describe to anyone who has not had the experience himself the unspeakable joy of watching the Lord as He works with fallible human beings, guiding them into something as precious as a dream fulfilled by God Himself? For

I had no doubt at all in my mind that what we were seeing—the university behind us and the ship in front of us—drew a shout of gladness and victory from the Lord Jesus Himself.

We had at last learned the greatest of all the lessons of guidance. It was exactly as Darlene had said earlier when she took my hand and whispered: "This is what hearing God is all about, isn't it, Loren? Getting to know Him better."

Flash Forward

SINCE the first edition of this book was printed, Loren Cunningham's dream of seeing waves of young people going out with the Gospel has continued to grow. Having recently passed its fortieth birthday, YWAM has established works in 950 locations in over 160 countries.

One of the most exciting trends is the speed of YWAM's growth among young people in the Third World. One in three of the twelve thousand full-time workers presently comes from countries that have traditionally been on the *receiving* end of missions.

Another important development has been the increasing commitment toward career missions. Short-term missionaries continue to go out, then recede like the waves of that early vision. Thirty thousand volunteered worldwide in a recent year in addition to more than two hundred thousand participants in short-term or specialized service (such as twenty thousand-plus in King's Kids International and three thousand in YWAM's Slavic Ministries).

More and more people are staying on, however, working on long-term projects of evangelism, church planting, relief and development, or training ministries. The multiplication that Loren and Darlene asked God for is happening, with a 7.5 percent annual growth rate in long-term staff over the past five years.

Many of the people mentioned in this book are still working to complete the Great Commission. Don Stephens continues to lead the Mercy Ships ministry of YWAM. Besides the *Anastasis*, there are two smaller ships in the mercy fleet. Don's goal is for ten ships to be ready to respond in any of the world's port cities with the two-handed Gospel of evangelism and practical aid.

Loren and Darlene press ahead for their lifelong goal: seeing the Gospel presented to every creature in this generation. While the growth of their dream has been phenomenal, they both realize it is still far short of all that God has put before them. For that to be fully accomplished, it will take many more miracles of multiplication, many more spiritual battles, and an ever attendant ear to hear their heavenly Father say...

This is the way...walk ye in it.

Twelve Points to Remember: Hearing the Voice of God

IF YOU know the Lord, you have already heard His voice—it is that inner leading that brought you to Him in the first place. Jesus always checked with His Father (John 8:26–29), and so should we. Hearing the voice of the heavenly Father is a basic right of every child of God. In this book we have tried to describe a few of many ways of fine-tuning this experience. The discoveries are never just theory. They come out of our own adventures:

1. Don't make guidance complicated. It's actually hard *not* to hear God if you really want to please and obey Him! If you stay humble, He promises to guide you (Prov. 16:9).

Here are three simple steps that have helped us to hear God's voice:

- *Submit* to His lordship. Ask Him to help you silence your own thoughts and desires and the opinions of others that may be filling your mind (2 Cor. 10:5). Even though you have been given a good mind to use, right now you want to hear the thoughts of the Lord, who has the best mind (Prov. 3:5–6).
- *Resist* the enemy, in case he is trying to deceive you at this moment. Use the authority that Jesus Christ has

given you to silence the voice of the enemy (James 4:7; Eph. 6:10–20).

- *Expect* an answer. After asking the question that is on your mind, wait for Him to answer. Expect your loving heavenly Father to speak to you. He will (John 10:27; Ps. 69:13; Exod. 33:11).

2. Allow God to speak to you in the way He chooses. Don't try to dictate to Him concerning the guidance methods you prefer. He is Lord—you are His servant (1 Sam. 3:9). Listen with a yielded heart; there is a direct link between yieldedness and hearing.

God may choose to speak to you through His *Word:* This could come in your daily reading, or He could guide you to a particular verse (Ps. 119:105); through an *audible voice* (Exod. 3:4); through *dreams* (Matt. 2) and *visions* (Isa. 6:1, Rev. 1:12–17). But probably the most common of all means is through the quiet *inner voice* (Isa. 30:21).

3. Confess any unforgiven sin. A clean heart is necessary if you want to hear God (Ps. 66:18).

4. Use the Axhead Principle—a term coined from the story in 2 Kings 6. If you seem to have lost your way, go back to the last time you knew the sharp, cutting edge of God's voice. Then obey. The key question is, *Have you obeyed the last thing God told you to do?*

5. Get your own leading. God will use others to confirm your guidance, but you should also hear from Him directly. It can be dangerous to rely on others to get the word of the Lord for you (1 Kings 13).

6. Don't talk about your guidance until God gives you permission to do so. Sometimes this happens immediately; at other times, there is a delay. The main purpose of waiting is to avoid four pitfalls of guidance: (a) *pride*, because God has spoken something to you; (b) *presumption*, by speaking before

you have full understanding; (c) missing God's *timing and method*; (d) bringing *confusion* to others; they, too, need prepared hearts (Luke 9:36; Eccles. 3:7; Mark 5:19).

7. Use the Wise Men Principle. Just as the Three Wise Men individually followed the star and, in doing so, were all led to the same Christ, so God will often use two or more spiritually sensitive people to *confirm* what He is telling you (2 Cor. 13:1).

8. Beware of counterfeits. Have you ever heard of a counterfeit dollar bill? Yes, of course. But have you ever heard of a counterfeit paper bag? No. The reason is that only things of value are worth counterfeiting.

Satan has a counterfeit for everything of God that is possible for him to copy (Acts 8:9–11; Exod. 7:22). Counterfeit guidance comes, for example, through Ouija boards, séances, fortune-telling, and astrology (Lev. 20:6; 19:26; 2 Kings 21:6). The guidance of the Holy Spirit leads you closer to Jesus and into true freedom. Satan's guidance leads you away from God into bondage.

One key test for true guidance: Does your leading follow principles of the Bible? The Holy Spirit never contradicts the Word of God.

9. Opposition of man is sometimes guidance from God (Acts 21:10–14). In our own story, we recognized much later that what seemed like blockage from our denomination was, in fact, God leading us into a broader scope of ministry. The important lesson here, again, is *yieldedness* to the Lord (Dan. 6:6–23; Acts 4:18–21). Rebellion is never of God, but sometimes He asks you to step away from your elders in a way that is not rebellion but part of His plan. Trust that He will show your heart the difference.

10. Every follower of Jesus has a unique ministry (1 Cor. 12; 1 Pet. 4:10–11; Rom. 12; Eph. 4). The more you seek to

hear God's voice in detail, the more effective you will be in your own calling. Guidance is not a game—it is serious business where we learn *what* God wants us to do in ministry and *how* He wants us to do it. The will of God is doing and saying the right thing in the right place, with the right people, at the right time, and in the right sequence, under the right leadership, using the right method, with the right attitude of heart.

11. Practice hearing God's voice and it becomes easier. It's like picking up the phone and recognizing the voice of your best friend—you know his voice because you have heard it so much. Compare young Samuel with the older man Samuel (1 Sam. 3:4–7; 8:7–10; 12:11–18).

12. Relationship is the most important reason for hearing the voice of the Lord. God is not only infinite but also personal. If you don't have communication, you don't have a personal relationship with Him. True guidance, as Darlene pointed out, is getting closer to the Guide. We grow to know the Lord better as He speaks to us, and as we listen to Him and obey, we make His heart glad (Exod. 33:11; Matt. 7:24–27).

Other Books by Loren Cunningham

WHY NOT WOMEN?
A Fresh Look at Scripture on Women in Missions, Ministry, and Leadership
> *by Loren Cunningham and David Joel Hamilton*, $14.99

Why Not Women? brings light, not just more heat, to the church's crucial debate with a detailed study of women in Scripture; historical and current global perspectives; an examination of the fruit of women in public ministry; and a hard-hitting revelation of what's at stake for women, men, the Body of Christ, God's Kingdom, and the unreached. (ISBN 1-57658-183-7)

MAKING JESUS LORD
The Dynamic Power of Laying Down Your Rights
> *by Loren Cunningham*, $9.99

We live in a world in which the protection and exaltation of individual rights has become an obsession. As Christians we believe that personal rights do hold great value. As a result, we can perform no greater act of faith and worship than to lay down these rights at the feet of the One who has gone before us, Jesus Himself! Loren Cunningham details proven steps to a transformed life of freedom, joy, and intimate fellowship with God. Includes study guide. (ISBN 1-57658-012-1)

DARING TO LIVE ON THE EDGE
The Adventure of Faith and Finances
> *by Loren Cunningham*, $9.99

Living by faith is not the domain of only those Christians called to "full-time" ministry. What is important is not our vocation, but whether we are committed to obeying God's will in our lives. If we are willing to step out in faith, doing whatever God has asked us to do, we will see His provision. A Christian who has experienced this is spoiled for the ordinary. (ISBN 0-927545-06-3)

Other Recommended Books
from YWAM Publishing

FOLLOWING JESUS
Attaining the High Purposes of Discipleship
> *by Ross Tooley,* $9.99

Following Jesus brings vision and direction to Christians who want to know God and make Him known. With straightforward teaching drawn from true stories of God's faithfulness and guidance, Ross Tooley examines how our passionate and patient God leads His present-day disciples into the dreams He has for them and for His Kingdom. (ISBN 1-57658-205-1)

SPIRITUAL WARFARE FOR EVERY CHRISTIAN
How to Live in Victory and Retake the Land
> *by Dean Sherman,* $12.99

God has called Christians to overcome the world and drive back the forces of evil at work within it. Spiritual warfare isn't just casting out demons; it's Spirit-controlled thinking and attitudes. Dean delivers a both-feet-planted-on-the-ground approach to the unseen world. With study guide. (ISBN 0-927545-05-5)

RELATIONSHIPS
The Key to Love, Sex, and Everything Else
> *by Dean Sherman,* $12.99

This refreshingly direct discussion of the often confusing world of love, sex, and relationships offers not another set of rules but the principles God has established for all relationships. Dean Sherman helps readers build their life relationships upon God's logical, loving, and freeing precepts. (ISBN 1-57658-275-2)

INTERCESSION, THRILLING AND FULFILLING
> *by Joy Dawson,* $12.99

This book proves that we are surrounded by opportunities to impact our world through the powerful means of intercessory prayer. *Intercession, Thrilling and Fulfilling* spells out the price of obedience but leaves us in no doubt that the rewards and fulfillment far outweigh that price. We become history shapers and closer friends of Almighty God. (ISBN 1-57658-006-7)

LEARNING TO LOVE PEOPLE YOU DON'T LIKE
How to Develop Love and Unity in Every Relationship

by Floyd McClung, $11.99

Does God really expect us to get along with each other? Floyd McClung offers challenging and practical answers for achieving productive, lasting relationships. Here is a firsthand account of how anyone can live in love and unity with others, both in the church and in the world. Includes study guide.
(ISBN 1-57658-380-5)

COURAGEOUS LEADERS
Transforming Their World

by James Halcomb, David Hamilton, and Howard Malmstadt,
$15.99

Our world needs courageous leaders who will recognize the need for God-motivated action and follow through with a God-led plan. Whether your vision for change is local or global, simple or complex, for home, business, or ministry, *Courageous Leaders* will help you remain on a true course and reach the goal set before you. (ISBN 1-57658-171-3)

THE LEADERSHIP PARADOX
A Challenge to Servant Leadership in a Power Hungry World

by Denny Gunderson, $11.99

What is the key to effective leadership? The ability to organize and take charge? The ability to preach and teach? Entrepreneurial skill? A charismatic personality? According to Jesus, none of the above. This refreshingly candid book draws us to the Master's side. Through the eyes of people who experienced Jesus firsthand, we discover insights that will challenge us to rethink our leadership stereotypes. Includes study guide.
(ISBN 1-57658-379-1)

DISCIPLING NATIONS
The Power of Truth to Transform Cultures, 2nd Edition

by Darrow Miller, $15.99

The power of the gospel to transform individual lives has been clearly evident throughout New Testament history. But what of the darkness and poverty that enslave entire cultures? In *Discipling Nations*, Darrow Miller builds a powerful and convincing thesis that God's truth not only breaks the spiritual bonds of sin and death but can free whole societies from deception and poverty. Excellent study of worldviews. Includes study guide. (ISBN 1-57658-015-6)

INTERNATIONAL ADVENTURES
Amazing True Stories of Spiritual Victory
and Personal Triumph

by various authors, $12.99 each

On every continent, in every nation, God is at work in and through the lives of believers. From the streets of Amsterdam to remote Pacific islands to the jungles of Ecuador and beyond, each international adventure that emerges is a dramatic episode that could be directed only by the hand of God...

Adventures in Naked Faith • ISBN 0-927545-90-X
Against All Odds • ISBN 0-927545-44-6
Bruchko • ISBN 1-57658-348-1
A Cry from the Streets • ISBN 1-57658-263-9
Dayuma: Life Under Waorani Spears • ISBN 0-927545-91-8
Imprisoned in Iran • ISBN 1-57658-180-2
Living on the Devil's Doorstep • ISBN 0-927545-45-4
Lords of the Earth • ISBN 1-57658-290-6
The Man with the Bird on His Head • ISBN 1-57658-005-9
Peace Child • ISBN 1-57658-289-2
Tomorrow You Die • ISBN 0-927545-92-6
Torches of Joy • ISBN 0-927545-43-8
Totally Surrounded • ISBN 1-57658-165-9

CHRISTIAN HEROES: THEN AND NOW
Great missionary biographies!

by Janet and Geoff Benge, $6.99 each
This popular series chronicles the exciting, challenging, and deeply touching true stories of ordinary men and women whose trust in God accomplished extraordinary exploits for His kingdom and glory. Inspiring true stories for ages 10 and up.

Gladys Aylward: The Adventure of a Lifetime • 1-57658-019-9
Nate Saint: On a Wing and a Prayer • 1-57658-017-2
Hudson Taylor: Deep in the Heart of China • 1-57658-016-4
Amy Carmichael: Rescuer of Precious Gems • 1-57658-018-0
Eric Liddell: Something Greater Than Gold • 1-57658-137-3
Corrie ten Boom: Keeper of the Angels' Den • 1-57658-136-5
William Carey: Obliged to Go • 1-57658-147-0
George Müller: The Guardian of Bristol's Orphans • 1-57658-145-4
Jim Elliot: One Great Purpose • 1-57658-146-2
Mary Slessor: Forward into Calabar • 1-57658-148-9
David Livingstone: Africa's Trailblazer • 1-57658-153-5
Betty Greene: Wings to Serve • 1-57658-152-7
Adoniram Judson: Bound for Burma • 1-57658-161-6
Cameron Townsend: Good News in Every Language • 1-57658-164-0
Jonathan Goforth: An Open Door in China • 1-57658-174-8
Lottie Moon: Giving Her All for China • 1-57658-188-8
John Williams: Messenger of Peace • 1-57658-256-6
William Booth: Soup, Soap, and Salvation • 1-57658-258-2
Rowland Bingham: Into Africa's Interior • 1-57658-282-5
Ida Scudder: Healing Bodies, Touching Hearts • 1-57658-285-X
Wilfred Grenfell: Fisher of Men • 1-57658-292-2
Lillian Trasher: The Greatest Wonder in Egypt • 1-57658-305-8
Loren Cunningham: Into All the World • 1-57658-199-3
Florence Young: Mission Accomplished • 1-57658-313-9
Sundar Singh: Footprints Over the Mountains • 1-57658-318-X
C.T. Studd: No Retreat • 1-57658-288-4
Rachel Saint: A Star in the Jungle • 1-57658-337-6
Brother Andrew: God's Secret Agent • 1-57658-355-4
Count Zinzendorf: Firstfruit • 1-57658-262-0
Clarence Jones: Mr. Radio • 1-57658-343-0

**Call 1-800-922-2143 for a full catalog,
or visit our website at www.ywampublishing.com**